To my Mot...
who has taught me
endlessly about
creativity
I Love you
chiquita

THE WELL OF
CREATIVITY

Quotes about Michael Toms

"...one of the best interviewers who has ever worked the American airwaves, radio or TV."
— Robert Fuller, physicist, educator, past president of Oberlin College, and active citizen diplomat

"Someone with whom I have cruised some important realms of the cosmic ocean and in doing so have developed ever-increasing confidence in his intuitive navigation."
— R. Buckminster Fuller (1895–1983), inventor of the geodesic dome; designer, philosopher, and creator of the World Games

"...Bill Moyers and Michael Toms are alike: two of the most creative interviewers it has been my good fortune to work with."
— Joseph Campbell (1904–1987), mythologist and author of *Hero with a Thousand Faces, The Masks of God, Myths to Live By,* and *The Mythic Image*

Please visit the Hay House Website at:
www.hayhouse.com
and the New Dimensions Website at:
www.newdimensions.org

THE WELL OF CREATIVITY

Julia Cameron
Natalie Goldberg
Deena Metzger
Keith Jarrett
Isabel Allende
and
Mihály Csikszentmihályi

WITH MICHAEL TOMS

Hay House, Inc.
Carlsbad, CA

Published and distributed in the United States by:
Hay House, Inc., P.O. Box 5100, Carlsbad, CA 92018-5100
(800) 654-5126 • (800) 650-5115 (fax)

Edited by Michael Toms, Rose Holland, and the Hay House editorial staff
Introductions, Prologues, and Epilogues by Michael Toms
Designed by: Jenny Richards

The authors of this book do not dispense medical advice or prescribe the use of any tech-nique as a form of treatment for physical or medical problems without the advice of a physician, either directly or indirectly. The intent of the authors is only to offer informa-tion of a general nature to help you in your quest for emotional and spiritual well-being. In the event you use any of the information in this book for yourself, which is your con-stitutional right, the authors and the publisher assume no responsibility for your actions.

Library of Congress Cataloging-in-Publication Data

The well of creativity / Julia Cameron and other contributors, with
   Michael Toms.
          p.   cm.
   Includes bibliographical references.
   ISBN 1-56170-375-3 (trade paper)
    1. Creative ability. 2. Creation (Literary, artistic, etc.)
3. Artists—Interviews.   I. Cameron, Julia.   II. Toms, Michael.
BF408.W42   1997
153.3'5—dc21   97-11927

ISBN 1-56170-375-3

00 99 98 97   4 3 2 1
First Printing, November 1997

Printed in the United States of America

New Dimensions Radio® is a registered trademark of New Dimensions Foundation.

CONTENTS

Editor's Note: Throughout the book, the interviewer's
questions are in italics.

PREFACE

About New Dimensions

New Dimensions Radio is the major activity of the New Dimensions Foundation, a nonprofit educational organization. "New Dimensions" is an international radio interview series featuring thousands of hours of in-depth dialogues on a wide variety of topics. **Michael Toms,** the co-founder of New Dimensions Radio, the award-winning host of the "New Dimensions" radio interview series—and a widely respected New Paradigm spokesperson and scholar himself—engages in thoughtful, intimate conversations with the leading thinkers and social innovators of our time, focusing on creative and positive approaches to the challenges of a changing society.

🔥　🔥　🔥

About This Book

Creativity is for everyone. Each of us has something creative to contribute, no matter what the task. This book brings together several views of creativity, including a filmmaker/composer, two writers, one who writes mostly nonfiction and the other mostly fiction, a psychotherapist/author, a musician/composer, and a psychologist. They all agree on one point: Creativity is accessible and available to each of us and can be found everywhere, even in the most mundane activities.

It is up to us to take up the baton and manifest our own creative symphony through whatever task we find meaningful.

INTRODUCTION

by Michael Toms

Whether you're an artist, stockbroker, or homemaker, being able to tap into your innate creativity enhances your life. Being creative means following your dreams and finding your life's purpose. You do not have to be trapped in the "dailyness" of your life and leave your passion behind. This book is about moving beyond the fear of failure and self-doubt, making the jump and taking the risk, and living at the creative edge and doing what you love.

Through the dialogues included here, you will get in touch with the great diversity inherent within the creative process. Practitioners, teachers, and researchers of the creative process are all represented here, and each has something important to say. The dynamic energy and enthusiasm of Julia Cameron is present in her words of wisdom about what it takes to be creative. Natalie Goldberg makes the important connection between spirituality and creativity. Deena Metzger tells us that through writing we can enter the depths within and become more whole. The legendary pianist, Keith Jarrett, reveals the magic and mystery inherent in the living moment where creativity resides. Isabel

Allende shows us the power of storytelling and how each of us has our own story. Mihály Csikszentmihályi gives us the benefit of a lifetime of research on creativity and creative persons, sharing many of the common traits that are part of being creative.

As each contributor to this book says, "Creativity is about discovery and hard work." Inspiration requires initiation and commitment to make it real in the world. You have a creative contribution to make. Your life and mine will be better if you do.

CHAPTER ONE

❦ ❦ ❦

Unlocking Your Creativity

Julia Cameron, with Michael Toms

PROLOGUE

*W*hether you're an artist, writer, banker, consultant, or a gardener, being able to tap into your inner creativity enhances your life. Being creative means following your dreams and finding your life's purpose. For whatever reason, most of us get trapped in the "dailyness" of our lives and leave our passion behind, or we become victims of our own fears of failure and self-doubt and are unable to make the jump and take the risk. This doesn't have to be the case.

Julia Cameron is an award-winning writer with extensive credits in film, television, theater, and journalism. Her essays have been anthologized twice, and she's published short fiction as well as criticism. She's also a published poet who teaches creative writing at the graduate level and who has taught creativity

*workshops for over a decade. She's co-author (with Mark Bryan)
of the bestseller,* The Artist's Way; *as well as the author of*
A Spiritual Path, The Higher Creativity, *and* The Vein of Gold:
A Journey to Your Creative Heart.

🔺   🔺   🔺

MICHAEL TOMS: *Julia, in your book* The Artist's Way, *and
also in* The Vein of Gold, *you see creativity as a spiritual process.
Can you elaborate on that?*

JULIA CAMERON: I think that it's a human process, and to be
human is to be spiritual. It's my experience that all of us are creative. It's not something that belongs to an elite few, and it's not
something that can be intellectually calibrated. For myself, I
don't make a distinction between being human, being spiritual,
and being creative. I think of this as our endowment.

*Often, we hold ourselves back. We see others as creative and
not ourselves. Why do you think that is?*

Well, we're very well trained to see other people as creative.
There is a very pervasive mythology that says that there are
geniuses, and then there are the rest of us—that artists are born
knowing they're artists, and they're sort of like armored salmon
that leap upstream and fend off anyone. We don't hear artists
speaking artist-to-artist very often. We hear artists talking to us
through the mechanism of the media. So we hear things such as:
"Steven [Spielberg] got his first movie camera at eight, and he
always knew he was going to be a film director." We don't hear
the stories about him sitting in a New York hotel room, discouraged and terrified, eating carry-out pizza and wondering if he
would ever be able to make *Close Encounters of the Third Kind.*

I was in that hotel room when I heard him be terrified, and all artists are often terrified. They simply learn to move through the fear, but the mythology that we have is that if we have fear around our creativity, we're not supposed to be doing it because fear means you're not a real artist.

It's like Susan Jeffers' book Feel the Fear and Do It Anyway. *Make fear your friend so you can move through it?*

Yes, and I think that a lot of the tools that I teach people have to do with them understanding the inner censor that says, "Who do you think you are? And what are the odds of your ever selling this book if you manage to write it? You'll never make a living at this. You're too old, and you're going to look like a total fool." That voice we take as the voice of reason, but actually it's an internalized wet blanket that dampens our creativity and tries to keep us from committing creativity. The tools that I teach allow people to hear that voice as a sort of cartoon character, like the wet-blanket relative to whom you say, "Let's do this, let's have a picnic," and he says, "It'll rain." Well, that's what we've internalized in terms of making art. We're always telling ourselves it's going to rain.

I know you put a lot of value on story, on our own story. I'm wondering about your story. How did you become a writer? Can you capsulize your own story for us?

I doubt it, but I'll try. I grew up in a big family. There were seven of us. We all wrote and drew and painted. It's often true if you're from a big family that creativity gets divvied up into fiefdoms. My older sister, Connie, is fantastic in music. So when I came along, music was sort of taken. One of the things that's very American is that we have a lug-bolt mentality around creativity.

We think if you're a writer you shouldn't be a painter. You shouldn't let yourself follow your creative itches. I know a lot about this because I happened to be a writer, because that was the available slot in my family. It took me years to realize that I'm a very good painter, just like my sister, Libby; and a very good composer, like my brother, Christopher. And that it was okay to have all of the gifts.

It's interesting how we have that seemingly in the West. A few years ago I visited Bali, and one of the things that really surprised me was that everybody in Bali does everything. Everybody does it.

Everybody does it. That's right, and that's because everybody can. That's what my tools are about. It's about "Wake up, you guys; we can all do this." Of course, it's a little anarchistic and anti-hierarchical. This is not what the art establishment would have us believe or even the studio system. You know, we're all supposed to believe that someone else is going to come along and tell us we're real artists. That if we're galleried, if we're published, if we're written up in the *New York Times,* that there's somewhere we're going to be able to get our passport stamped, and it's going to say "Artist," and everybody will have to believe it.

The thing that I know after 30 years is that you just make things, and it is the act of making things that A, makes you happy, which is another thing we aren't told. B, it makes you an artist, and that even when you have all the credentials in the world, you will still sometimes have those nights where you don't know you're an artist. So you have to learn to do it any-way. You need to learn to know that mood does not matter. It's like sex. You can think, *I'm not interested,* but once you begin, you may find out it's more interesting. It's the same thing with creativity. If we keep waiting for the perfect mood, we're going to end up starved.

This might be a good time to go into one of your tools. One of your techniques is the morning pages. Could you talk about the morning pages?

Morning pages are, I like to say, a Western form of meditation, because most of us hate sitting there. So what you do is you get up in the morning, and that's why they're called morning pages, and you write three pages of longhand writing about anything. It literally is, "Boy, the window sills are really filthy. I hate the traffic on this street. I think that Carol stole credit for my idea in the meeting yesterday. I didn't call my sister back." It's that kind of thing.

So it's stream of consciousness?

It's stream of consciousness, or another way to put it is "stream of gripe." Stream of worry. Stream of preoccupation.

And don't use the word processor to do this, right?

Well, everybody cheats sooner or later, but my experience—and most of the people that I have worked with have found this—is that there is something in the hand itself, moving across a page, that slows us down, grounds us, and allows us to contact our truth more clearly than using the word processor. On the other hand, if for some reason you cannot write using a pen or a pencil, use a word processor.

This brings out the question—and you've written about this—the question being that most of us feel we don't have enough time to be creative.

The favorite thing is, "Well, Julia, I do not have enough time to do morning pages, they must take 45 minutes." What morning pages do is tell you the kind of day you want to have. They prioritize your day. They make you understand very clearly where you are giving your time away to other people's agendas. They teach you when you are falling in with all of the "shoulds." I should do this. I ought to do that. Never asking yourself what would I passionately love to have done today. Sometimes the answer is one 15-minute walk. So morning pages give you a day. If you do them at night, you're complaining about the day you've already had. Morning pages lay down track, and they win you enormous windows of time. They also train your censor to stand to one side. So when you start writing, and your censor starts saying, "You're griping, you're negative, you're this, you're that," you say, "Thank you very much for sharing. Stay to the left and keep writing."

What this means is that as you move through your day, this is a transferable skill, so that you will find that you do everything with less procrastination. The objection will come up and you'll say, "Just a minute; I'm going to do this." So you gain enormous amounts of time that way. I love that question.

Well, this all brings to mind, too, the worry that comes up and says, "Well, I've got these other things to do. I've got appointments today." So how long does it usually take you to do the morning pages?

I'm a whip. I've been doing them for millions of years. I drink cold coffee. I'm a fanatic. 15 minutes. But they probably start out taking 45, and people get quicker as they become more and more accustomed to simply moving their hand across the page rapidly. At first when you start to do them, it can be like my longtime teaching partner, Mark Bryan, says: "We don't stare into space; we stare into time." So people will be writing, and something will hit them, and they'll be staring into space. I find if you set a little buzzer or something, you stare into space less. If you give yourself less time to do the pages, you'll get them done. Does that make sense to you?

Yes, it does. Is there a time to write? Is there a time to be creative, or can you be creative anytime?

Oh, anytime. I didn't even understand the question for a minute because this is another thing that morning pages do, is teach you, I call it, dropping down the well or walking across the bridge into what I call the imagic-nation. It can be done anywhere. I've written musicals and films flying back and forth on airplanes. I've done it waiting in a doctor's office.

On napkins in restaurants.

Napkins in restaurants, anywhere. Creativity is portable because we're portable. It doesn't have to be a special space, a special time. We simply need to get more and more facile at connecting into it. That's what these tools teach.

What about the artist date?

If you want to think of it as a radio set, with the morning pages you're sending. You're notifying the universe that this is what I like, this is what I don't like, and this is what I want. With the artist date, you're receiving. You go out once a week, and you do something festive and preplanned. So the words *artist* and *date* are both relevant. It's a *date*. You make it with yourself, with your own creative consciousness. You do not take children or spouses, and you do something interesting and expansive for yourself. Art is an image-using system, so in order to draw from that well, we have to consciously keep that ecosystem stocked.

What you do with artist dates is you turn the dial so that you are on receive. You let images in. If people do morning pages and don't do the artist date, they're like somebody who is on a life raft in the middle of the sea, sending "Here I am. Here I am. Here I am." And never flicks it over to the other channel where the big boat can say, "Okay, I'm trying to work with you, but tell me again where you are." So you need to use both tools so you receive as well as send.

One of the techniques that you write about for sparking one's creativity is the process of simply walking. Can you talk about walking?

I think this is the vastly overlooked creative tool of our time. We say things such as, "I'm walking myself back into my creativity," or "I'm trying to walk myself into a new career." We never stop to think that this is literal. One of the things that I have found is if people will walk 20 minutes a day anywhere, what begins to happen is that walking moves us into our body, and when we are in our body, we are in our breath. The word is *inspired. Inspiration.*

When people walk, they begin to enter what shamans would call an altered state, where you have an expanded sense of self and of connection. It's at once very large, and very particular. It is often on walks that you will integrate a problem, or if you have a tangled plot line as a writer, you'll suddenly see a new solution. Lots of us intuitively do this. If our relationship is getting dreadful, we go for long walks. Well, it's also true that if you go for enough walks, your relationships might not get quite so dreadful because you put things into a different, a higher perspective. It's an enormously potent tool. I do not think I can say enough about it. People really need to just try it for a couple of weeks. That's usually sufficient for them to notice.

I think of the Native American shamanic tradition of the vision quest. You walk into the desert going on retreat. It's always been walking to wherever you're going to retreat to.

That's right. We have always walked as a people. We have simply forgotten it in our culture.

There's also something about walking on the earth that connects you to the earth energies that you don't otherwise experience.

When you walk, you are able to hear more cleanly and more keenly. In my opinion, life is about listening. It is about listening to ourselves. It is about listening to our greater selves. It's about listening to the things that we hear with what you might call our "inner ears." The word *heart* has the word *ear* in the center of it. Also, it has the word *art* in the center of it. When we walk, we begin to be able to hear with the ears in our hearts. We begin to learn from our landscape. Sometimes we learn simply what we don't want, if we're in a cacophonous environment.

But I find, again, this is where I value a piece of music such as Tim Wheater's "Green Dreams," or another piece of Wheater's music called "Timeless." When you're in a very busy environment, if you listen to certain pieces of music and walk, they will take you across the bridge to knowing yourself in a larger and deeper way. Walking tends to give us self-respect. Part of this is American. This is the work ethic, and if you did nothing else today, at least I did my walk. At least I did my morning pages. But I also think it gives us self-respect, because we become grounded. We walk on the ground, and we become grounded. We contact our souls quite literally through the soles of our feet. The book *Vein of Gold* is dedicated to my artist daughter and to her grandparents, her ancestors. One of the things that we find when we walk is that we are able to hear the wisdom of people who have gone before us. We are connected in a much broader sense to the earth and also to ourselves.

Sound healer Don Campbell says something very interesting. He talks about all song beginning with the motion of the body. One the things that I have found is that if we will move, if we will walk, we will be able to walk ourselves into our souls and literally walk ourselves into our songs. I mean that term very literally. If you think about notes as being very similar to words, words are a trail, a series of choices that say, "I think this. I thought this. I was here at that time." Notes do the same thing. One of the things we do not say is that we are essentially musical beings. All of us. We, in order to have sound lives, must be immersed in sound, and the note that we are straining to hear is what I call our "own true note." Each of us has a song.

It's interesting that *note* rhymes with *vote* and that when we are being particularly true to ourselves, we speak from a central point that allows us to communicate to each other without anger, without coercion, without less than or more than. It's a very clear tone, and when we use it, people hear us.

I was just reading about a scientific experiment on babies and music, and the experiment showed that young infants had more resonance with harmonics than they did with dissonant kinds of sounds. The babies would turn to the speaker and would cry or just be upset. It's interesting that we may come in with that natural resonance with musical sounds.

I used to sing to my daughter, Dominica, when she was tiny. I used to do little jazz riffs with her. She remembers these 15 years later even though she was three months old. I sang one a couple of years ago, and all of a sudden she lit up and said, "Mommy, that's my song." I hadn't sung it to her since she was about three months old.

One of the things that touched me in Vein of Gold *was that you mentioned being sung to with the Irish lullaby "Turra Lurra Lurra." I remember that as a child, too, in my Irish family. It was such a wonderful lullaby, and it just brought back the healing quality and the sense of loving and the sense of being held.*

I hope that people will learn from the *Vein of Gold* how to hold themselves. The first kingdom is the kingdom of story, where they go back and retrieve those memories. Oh yes, I did have a lullaby. Many of the tools that I like to work with are what people might call children's tools. So people tend to want to resist them intellectually. Where is this going to get me? So I usually tell intellectuals, "Don't worry, it's Zen." I tell the rest of them, "Don't worry, it's fun."

Now I sense from your writings and your work that what you're doing comes out of being. I think this is a salient issue in our culture and in our times—the difference between being and doing. We tend to live in a doing culture. Doing is first. Then we can have, and then we can be. It really needs to start with being, doesn't it? What do you think?

I believe that we are intended to be in the moment and that we are intended to make things. That the joy is in the process and not in the product. That we're all exhausted from trying to be finished products and turning out well. When will I be okay? This is why we need to play, because when we play, we end up making things in the moment that are, in fact, eternal.

It's amazing how we get conditioned, and we get tracked out and we don't listen. We don't pay attention to what's really important. We get tracked out about what we think is important.

That's right (singing) "The mind is a limited faculty, a bright lamp with no shade. Get transcendentally mental, and no one makes the grade. The mind without emotion is a head without a horse. Doesn't pay to be rational when you steer a course. There is no logical reason for that pothole to appear. You'll be modeled by all potholes, till you let intuition steer." You see, we have stopped listening to our larger mind, which is embodied. We have it backwards.

Julia, one of the things you also talk about is a tool called the "creative cluster," and I think this is important because we tend to get isolated. Can you talk a little bit about the cluster?

In a perfect world, we would grow up in families who would listen to our dreams and say, "I'll bet you can do that, and I can probably help you, and here's how." But often our families are frightened by our dreams. They're worried that we're not going to be able to make money at them, so they start trying to shape our dreams in sensible directions. So part of what we do as adults when we begin to take ourselves more seriously, which means when we begin to think we might be allowed to play, is that we need to look around and think, *Who do I know who is positive, festive, supportive, and resilient?* You ask that person to be a sort of running buddy for you around your creativity.

One of the things that I'm very pleased about is that there are clusters all over the world working *the artist's way*. I have people coming up and saying, "Well, we were in a Panamanian jungle and we met every Sunday night, and it used to rain through the thatched roof," or "I had a little cluster in the middle of the outback."

There is something I want to say. Christ wasn't kidding. Wherever two or more are gathered, there is a power in the midst of them. If you want to talk about it in terms of neo-paganism, you would say you can raise quite a cone of power. If you want to intellectualize it, you can call it a think tank. But what it really is, is drawing together tribally in order to manifest our dreams with more potency. It's a sort of safety net, on the one hand, if you get discouraged.

For example, when I sang that little snippet of song, I got terrified and kind of mortified and went, *Oh my God, Julia.* One of the things that my cluster would do would be saying, "Oh, it was fine. Lighten up, it was good, you know." They were just a little shocked that it was a song. So your cluster says to you, "Try another gallery. Send it out again. Couldn't you do it this way?" I ask people to gather together with luminous hearts for each other and to meet and to work these tools as clusters. They're very playful, but they're very strong. So people can sometimes be either A, frightened; or B, discouraged, if they try to do them alone. Pilgrims used to always go in groups. I mean, yes, we can go out alone into the desert to think and seek our answers, but we can also walk and dance our way to the other side. It's more fun if we do it together.

Later, in The Vein of Gold, *you refer to the creative snipers.*

They are the people who, when you think about writing a book, say, "Oh, what are your odds of getting it published anyway?!" Or you give them an advance copy of your book and they say, "Do you know that there are typos on page 48 and 48?" You're thinking, *That's all that you got from the first 50 pages that took me a decade to write?* Creative snipers are usually people whom you are threatening because you are raising your own creative ceiling, which suggests that they might be able to raise theirs. Snipers are always telling you things "for your own good," but it's really for their own comfort.

So what do you do with that criticism? Just ignore it?

I went to the American Booksellers Association convention, and I sang a lot of *Avalon,* a musical that I wrote. Later I got a letter from a lady who said, "Your music is exquisite. Your songs are exquisite, but your gnarled hair and your rumpled suit, I do not approve of." I read this letter and I thought, *What do I do with this?* I called a girlfriend and said, "Could I please have a reality check?" She said, "You didn't look gnarled and rumpled, and your suit was lovely. Why don't you burn the letter?" So I burned it. When I took the action of saying, "This is completely unacceptable and nuts and inaccurate, and I will burn it," it put me back into a sense of this is not a hostile universe. This is a universe where I have a few choices.

So you really transformed it by burning it?

Usually what I do is write wicked little songs about it. Art is an alchemical process, and one of the best things that we can do when we have a blow to our creativity or a blow in any area, is to make some piece of art of it. Whether you collage images about how it made you mad. Whether you do a little rhymed ditty. Whether you write a song about it. Whether you paint about it. In order to recuperate from a couple of decades in Hollywood, I wrote a very funny bunch of short stories. That was my way of pulling the thorns out, and, you know, all of us can do this. It's more productive to bake a pie about an issue than it is to brood over and try and be adult and try and distance ourselves.

I think that's good advice. I want to go back to Avalon. *I know that your contemporary work has taken you into sound, and, of course, one of the chapters in* The Vein of Gold *is "The Kingdom of Sound," and how listening is so important to cre-*

ativity. Maybe you can talk a little bit about your work now, working with sound and sound healing.

For me, this was a great mystery. I come from a musical family, but I had always been told by teachers that I was a bad alto. Turns out I'm a soprano—no wonder I can't sing it low. About three years ago, I was doing my morning pages, and I got this idea: Wouldn't it be fun to do a musical about Merlin? The answer was yes, if I were musical. Then another month later, it was: You will be writing radiant songs. I thought, *Well, I'm 45 years old, and if I were to be writing radiant songs, it would have already happened.* But I have learned to listen to this voice, which you can call intuition or the still, small voice or whatever you want to call it.

So when I had the urge to go to England, it didn't make any sense to me, but I went. When I got there, it was literally as if music were hanging in the air for me. I wrote a musical. Because I played no instrument, I had to write it with my voice. I devised an alphabet system on a little teeny synthesizer, literally a-b-c-d, and I would listen to the music coming through my head, and I would find the notes, and I would write it out in alphabet code, which later moved over to notation. I now have written two musicals. I thought this was impossible.

When I was in my twenties, I worked in Washington and wrote for the *Washington Post*. One of my friends is a man who now, 30 years later, is the *Washington Post* music critic emeritus. He listened to *Avalon,* and he said, "My God, you have such melodic gift. I didn't know that." It was above my creative ceiling. It was something I believed I could not do. This is what I most want to say to people about their dream—that if there is something that you are passionately in love with and wish you could do, the odds are perhaps you can, and that, like me, you are simply very afraid of trying it.

Do you think that anything is possible?

Yes. That's the scary part. That's the part we're responsible for. You know, I had all the clues for years. I would always write that it would be lovely to be a torch singer next time. A musician next time. Then I didn't have to try and do it this time. Now that I'm doing it this time, I'm so much happier. So much more terrified.

And you can do something else next time.

It might be fun to just *be* music.

Why is it, do you think, that we procrastinate so much? We may have all this talent, all this creativity, yet we hold ourselves back, we procrastinate. Why is that?

We're scared, and we want things to be perfect. We don't know how to do baby steps. We want it to be safe. What we profoundly want is to be safe. We don't understand that being in our creativity is what makes us safe. We think not doing it is what makes us safe. When *The Artist's Way* came out, therapists all over America started using it. Their clients started getting better in droves, and it's because a lot of what we think of as neurosis in this country is simply people who are very unhappy because they're not using their creative endowment. I think most of us are far healthier than our 70-year-old paradigm of therapy would tell us.

It's kind of a different screen, a job, and having your work. Following your passion with your work. Or having a job.

No. You see, people believe that they have to change their entire life to be happy. If we change little teeny pieces every day, we get happier. Often the last thing we change is the big job. By the time we change it, we've invented the new job one little tiny piece at a time. Mark Bryan, whom I taught with for a long, long time, used to say that people think they have to blow their lives up. They have to dismantle everything. We get very dramatic because then we can stay blocked. If we make it so dramatic, we can't make the change. So I try to tell people to just do a little thing. You know, writing *Avalon,* I did it one note at a time. One song at a time. Now, I've written 70 songs, and I know it can be done. But if I had looked up and said, "Okay, you're going to have to learn how to notate music," if I had looked up instead of just taking the next footfall, would I have done it? This is why we need to walk. It teaches us to do it one beat at a time.

Just fall into it. Let it happen. I wonder why we don't let life unfold. We have this desire to want to control it. We have this illusion that we can control it, and it prevents us from just letting it happen.

We try to control the parts that we can't, and we refuse to control the parts that we can, right? If we allow ourselves to make things, to make a little piece of art, to write a lullaby, to take a wounding situation and do a nasty little poem about it, when we take that kind of power, we discover that we have an enormous capacity to make coarse adjustments in our life. We pretend that we're powerless. We are not powerless. We need to listen. The musical I'm writing now is called *Magellan.* He was the greatest navigator of his time. You might say, you're powerless; either there's wind or there isn't. But if there isn't much, and you knew how to work with what you've got, you can go a long ways. What we're trying to do with all these tools is listen for the direction in which it is possible to make movement.

It reminds me of a story that Joseph Campbell told me once. It was a story about someone coming up to him, a student or someone who attended one of his lectures. And the person said, "Professor Campbell, you've written so many books. How did you do that? How could you have written so many books?" And he paused for a moment and he said, "Well, write every day for 40 years, and you'll have written a lot of books, too."

Yes. That's the whole trick, right? Doing it a little bit at a time. Doing it all the time. Not making it a special occasion. In the last three years, I've written *Avalon,* I've written most of *Magellan.* I wrote *The Vein of Gold.* I have a book of short stories. It does help to teach creativity. This is why people should do clusters, because it reminds you of when you're getting in your own way. Selfishly, I teach in order to stay unblocked myself, because when I am unblocked and doing my work, I'm very happy.

🔺　🔺　🔺

EPILOGUE

The message here is that creativity is available to all of us. We need only reach for it. Choose it. Embrace it. Each of us is unique and has original gifts to offer the world. Life is too brief not to follow our passion and live in the fullness of our creativity. Julia Cameron reminds us that we are not dependent on external acknowledgment to be creative, but rather it is our natural birthright, and we are the only ones who can release it or hold it back. Cameron believes that one of the ways to connect with the greater spirit of the world is through our creativity. No traditional concept of God is necessary to succeed, only a sense that our personal creativity reflects that of the universe, and as we express our artistic impulses we come in touch with a spiritual world of infinite size and power. No matter what your age or life path, whether being a creative artist is your career, your hobby, or your dream; it is not too late, too egotistical, too selfish, or too silly to work on your creativity.

CHAPTER TWO
❧ ❧ ❧

Creativity As Spiritual Practice

Natalie Goldberg, with Michael Toms

PROLOGUE

*W*riting can take you to a place inside yourself—the true
source of creative power. Few of us appear willing to make
the investment, even though most of us harbor a secret flotilla of
writing ambitions. Natalie Goldberg believes that all of us can
write—we simply have to do it. Natalie is an award-winning poet,
Zen practitioner, and teacher of writing workshops across the
country. She presents a larger vision of the writer's task: balanc-
ing the demands of daily life with the commitment to writing,
learning to cross boundaries both as a writer and human being,
dealing with success and failure, learning self-acceptance, and
withstanding the pain of endings in both art and life. She is the
author of the bestselling books, Writing Down the Bones, Wild
Mind: Living the Writer's Life, Long Quiet Highway, *and the
novel,* Banana Rose.

🐝   🐝   🐝

MICHAEL TOMS: *Natalie, when did writing begin for you? When do you remember starting it as a craft?*

NATALIE GOLDBERG: I remember pretty clearly that it was when I was 24 years old. I never thought of writing before that. I was an English Lit major in college, and I was madly in love with literature all through high school. But it never dawned on me that I could write, partially because we never read any women authors. They were all dead, from 17th-century England. When I was 24, I owned a restaurant called Naked Lunch. It was the first natural foods restaurant in Ann Arbor, Michigan. I was making ratatouille one day, and in order to make it for restaurants, I was cutting eggplants and onions all day long. I walked home at night, and I stopped in Center Core Bookstore and looked through the books, and there was a thin volume called *Fruits and Vegetables,* by Erica Jong. I opened it and it was about cooking an eggplant. I thought, *Wow, you can write about something like that. That ordinary something I do.* I must have been ready all along, and some synapse closed. I shut the book, and I said to myself, "Well, then, I'm going to write. I'm going to write about my family because nobody could tell me I'm wrong. I know them better than anyone else."

Then what happened? You just started writing about your family?

I started writing about my family, and one thing led to another. My motto has always been "Follow what you love, and it'll take you where you need to go." So that's what happened. I went back to school, got a teaching certificate, taught English, and started developing a writing practice.

Your roots have been important to you, and you've written about them—particularly your family roots. There was a really touching story that you told about making a pilgrimage to see your grandmother. Could you tell us about her?

My grandmother meant a lot to me. She was with me during my whole childhood. She lived in the same house and told me stories at night. I just adored her. Through my grandmother and grandfather, I learned what love was. Just simply love. Not a big deal. Not anything to it—it's just there. It's natural. If you stop carrying on, it's just there, and it's meant to be. My grandmother ended up in a nursing home in her old age—the horror of all Americans. Here was my grandmother whom I loved so much, and she was in a nursing home on Long Island. Then my parents and all the relatives ended up moving to Florida, retiring. Suddenly she was left alone there. At 94, she was blind and senile, and she had a diaper on. She was alone there.

I was living in Minnesota then, and when I said I wanted to go visit her, my parents said, "Oh, she won't remember anything." I think they were very defensive because it was painful for them. She won't know you, and it doesn't matter. So finally I thought, *I can't listen to that. I have to trust myself,* and I didn't have a lot of money then. I flew in, and I made the journey just to go see her at the nursing home. It was the Polly Patterson Nursing Home on Long Island. I pulled up, went in, and there she was. Nobody had been there to see her in years. She was toothless. This was my grandmother. The woman I loved so much. I just climbed into bed with her. She didn't know who I was, but there was so much love.

After being with her for a long time, she suddenly, for a moment, became completely cognizant. We were singing a song together that we sang when I was a young girl. The world just felt perfect. I felt like, No, she didn't live past her time as my relatives had said. This was her time. It was a very deep experience. I was so happy that she was still alive. Since then, I've visited her several times, although it seemed like she didn't know me or anything. Once another friend came with me and took some photos. I have a photo of my grandmother and me. There's just beaming love in the photograph. You'd never know that she was blind and senile and all the other stuff.

When you first started writing, did you set out to write a book? Did you have a goal in mind?

No. I had no goal. See, I was very lucky. I had no goals. It's like I stepped out of the world and just wrote. I just kept writing. I filled notebooks. I wrote poems. I was a poet for 13 years. Being a poet in America is having no career, having no credentials. It's like a Zen monk. So that's where I really developed.

What was it like to be a poet for 13 years? How did you support yourself?

People ask me that, but luckily it was the hippie years. So the New Age culture supported my life as a poet. You didn't care about money. I moved to Taos and lived in a house with dirt floors, and I chopped wood and had an outhouse for four years for $15 a month. It was then that I developed my writing practice. I didn't really care about money. I didn't think about it. I was happy I was writing. It was a deep dream that I never even knew was a dream.

What's happened since you've become more well known or famous, as it were, with the success of your books? Has that changed your life in any way?

I've taken my phone listing out of the phone book. I've had to deal with it. Some of it was very difficult. People project on you their idea of being famous. As I kept telling them, it's another American dream. It's not that big a deal. It's actually painful. It isolated me further. It was lonely. I had to deal with everybody's projections on me. What it does do for me, and this is very empirical, I make a living now as a writer. I get to write other books that get published, and people read them. That's it, and that's wonderful. But we imbue it with so much more than that. It doesn't do any of that. I named what it does.

You want to name it again so everybody gets it?

You get to get your book published. You get to get other books published. You get to make a living as a writer. And people read your writing. That's it, and that's actually quite wonderful in itself. Just like drinking a glass of water. It's wonderful to drink a glass of water. We don't have to make it that this water comes from the middle of the earth and on and on. What it is, is enough in itself.

Natalie, you were mentioning people projecting on you and their writing dreams or how you're supposed to be if you're a famous writer. Why do you think there's this fascination in America with writers and writing? There are magazines published about writing. There are new books all the time about writing. Why is that?

There's incredible romance around writing, it's true. I think underneath it all, everybody has a longing to express themselves. To connect with themselves. To write, you have to have a relationship with your own mind. Now people don't consciously realize that, but I think they feel that unconsciously. Everybody wants to connect with themselves in a society that is so alienated. There's a lot of loneliness in our society. People are longing to connect with themselves, and they don't know how. They see writing as a way to do it. It is amazing. It's just amazing. In every walk of life, I meet people who tell me they've always wanted to write. What I've done is make it very empirical. No big deal. This is how you do it. It's simple, but it's not easy.

What advice would you give to someone who has always wanted to be a writer? How does one begin to be a writer?

You get a pen, a fast writing pen. Get a cheap notebook. Nothing fancy, so you can write a lot of junk in it and just start. Say, okay, I'm going to write ten minutes three times a week. When you start that ten minutes, you keep your hand going. Write anything you want for ten minutes. Writing is an athletic activity. We don't realize that. We would never expect to go for our first tennis lesson and then play Wimbledon the next day. We sit down to start writing, and we expect our first word on the page to be the beginning of *War and Peace*. We allow practice in other areas, other athletic endeavors. We need to understand that writing is an athletic endeavor and that we need to practice before we write a book.

I sense from reading your material that writing is almost a spiritual practice for you. I want to make the connection. There is a connection between the spiritual practice that you follow and your writing, isn't there?

It is the same thing. I studied with Katagiri Roshi, and after I was studying with him for three or four years, he said, "Why don't you make writing your practice? If you go all the way with the writing, it'll take you everyplace Zen does. Anything you commit yourself to completely you'll have to face."

So it's really a spiritual practice. That's what it is, number one, before I write a book, before I do anything. I don't just finish one book and quit. I have to continue under all circumstances. So I write book after book, and I practice. I continue.

In the beginning, I remember I had just come from studying with Chögyam Trungpa Rinpoche in Boulder, Colorado. It was a tremendous amount of pomp and circumstance. You had to make an appointment a year in advance and get all dressed up. When I moved to Minneapolis, I knew I was a Buddhist and that I would study with any Buddhist teacher who was in the area. It was Katagiri Roshi. I called the Zen center, and I asked to make an appointment, thinking that I could see him in a year. It was a man on the other end with a Japanese accent, and he said come right over. I drove over, and I got all dressed up.

When I walked into the Zen center, I realized that it was him on the phone. He greeted me in jeans and a green T-shirt that said "Marcy School is Purr-fect," and there was a cat on it. It was his son's elementary school. We sat down and I chatted a little bit, and I was very unimpressed. I thought to myself, *He's very boring.* I missed all the glitter. I kept going to practice, but I knew I didn't really care about him. I was very arrogant.

About a month later, Nancy James, who was running the newsletter at the Zen center, called me and asked if I would go interview Roshi for the next newsletter. I said okay. So the next day I made an appointment. I woke up that morning obsessed with what color curtains to get for my house. I just got married, and I thought, *Oh, what a bother to go interview Roshi. I'll go interview him and then run and get the curtains.* So I dashed over, and my mind was just roaring. Should they be yellow? Should they be orange?

I pulled up in front of Zen center, and I dashed out, and then I'd forgotten my notebook. So I ran back to the car, got my notebook, ran into the Zen center, whipped around the corner, and there was Roshi in full robes watering one flower. He was completely watering that flower with every cell in his body. I just stopped dead. I pointed at the flower and I said, "Roshi." It was a flower that someone had brought from Hawaii about a month before for a wedding. I just pointed and said "Roshi." He turned and smiled and said, "Yes. When you take care of something, it lasts a long time." That was my first real meeting with him. Then I saw who he really was. From then on, I studied with him intensely for six years. Then I moved to New Mexico, and he was still my teacher. I kept writing, and the writing is what took me deeply into understanding him.

What do you think Roshi meant when he said to go all the way with your writing?

I think it means give it 100 percent, heart and soul. You know, nothing stops you. Great determination. Under all circumstances, don't be tossed away. You make a commitment to it. This is your path. Whether you get published or whether you don't, it doesn't matter.

You went back to be with him when he was dying, too, didn't you?

Yes, I did. He died March 1, 1990. I went to say good-bye to him because I had to leave for two months while he was sick in bed. He never said this before. He said, "I'll see you again." I thought, *Oh, he knows something I don't know.* Then he did die. I tried to get there before he died, but I wasn't able to. I was in Taos. I flew in that night, and he had died that morning. I arrived at the zendo at 10:30 that night and sat with the body for three days. I sat at the ovens while he was cremated, and about 15 minutes before it was done, I was able to look in the oven, and there were just a few ribs left of my great teacher and probably the most important person in my life.

Natalie, in both Writing Down the Bones *and* Wild Mind, *you have some exercises. One of the things you did in* Wild Mind *is you shared seven rules of writing, beginning with "keep your hand moving." What do you mean by "keep your hand moving"?*

Once you say *go,* if you commit yourself to ten minutes of writing, you keep your hand moving. You don't stop, you don't pause, you don't think. Just whatever you can think of, just keep that hand moving. It cuts through resistance. It separates out the editor and creator. One of our problems is that we mix them up so that while we're trying to create, the editor is tapping at our shoulder saying, "Don't do that. Don't say this." We freeze. So it's a way of separating it out. It's the practice, like in Zen practice. When the bell rings, you sit still for 40 minutes no matter what comes up. With writing, you keep your hand moving no matter what.

One of the things you said was to write your first thought. It reminds me that the first thought usually is the one that says, "Oh, no, no, you can't put that on paper."

That's true, but first thoughts are where the real power and the real energy is. Usually our first thought might be something like "Drop dead." Our second thought might be, "Oh, what a lovely dress you're wearing."

In our culture, we're very rarely exposed to first thoughts, so maybe that's why they do sound and come off so fully alive— because they're so rare.

They're from the bottom of the mind before our human life moves in. So they're very raw and alive and full of energy.

What does it mean, that you "don't think when writing"?

Usually our thinking is a way we're trying to get control of it. Our thinking is usually that this stinks. This is awful. I hate this. Just don't try to be logical. Just allow writing to go where it goes. From doing it you begin to understand your mind, and you realize you're not in control of your mind. If you step out of the way, your mind has things to say that are actually clear and whole, but they don't seem logical.

What about the writing that requires reference to facts and events and things like that?

You could throw that in. That's fine.

But don't you have to think in that process?

Yes, but when I say "thinking," usually people do thinking that's like thoughts on thoughts. A way to control things. To grab a first thought like lemon and put down "lemon." Instead, we go lemon, oh, we think it should be more artistic. Lemon like the sun. We have to cogitate and make it very self-conscious.

I'm reminded of something one of the Tibetan teachers once said. It's not the thoughts; it's the thinking of the thoughts that's the problem.

Yes. That's wonderful. Yes, that's it. It's thought on thought. Your first thought is whole and fine, let it be. But we have to grab it and try to manipulate it.

It's interesting how our minds work that way. It's like we might have been sitting quiet, reflecting, and suddenly there's a thought. Then we're off and running somewhere, and we catch ourselves and say, "Gee, how did I get off over there? I was just here."

Another rule is lose control. Lose control, or say what you really want to say, not what you think you should say. We're all control freaks.

Why do you think that is, that we're all control freaks?

I think because we're afraid of the way things really are. The way things really are is that it's impermanent, and there's nothing we can hold on to. Our human ego wants to eat things up—make a solid world. We forget that we're going to die.

And what about "be specific"?

Oh, that's wonderful. That keeps you grounded on the earth. It's not a car; it's a Cadillac. It's a Ford. It's a pomegranate. It's a sycamore. It's real things on the earth. We don't dream, even in the abstract.

In some ways, our educational system is built on abstractions.

I'm afraid so, and that's why we're losing so many kids. Kids are alive and vital now. They're really bored, and they go to sleep. I've lost many, many hours in school. That's what we do when we read a poem in school. We read the poem, and then we abstract rather than feel the vitality of what that writer is writing about. We step away from the heat of words, and say this poem is about justice. And finally, it really makes it boring.

How would you engage the vitality of a poem? What would be some suggestions for children in a classroom?

I would read it aloud, then just sit with the vibrancy of it. Maybe just point out and repeat lines we really liked. Then, I'd have kids do a recall. Okay, recall anything you remember as close as you can to the way that the author wrote it. Then they take on the voice of the author. That's really what writing is about. Literature is really moments of inspiration that are passed on. So what we pass on is the breath of inspiration.

This might be a good time to read something from the book Long, Quiet Highway.

Okay. I thought maybe I'd read about one of my teachers, since the book is about teachers and leads up to my Zen teacher. But this is about my French teacher in high school:

> Where were the women teachers? Remember the times—the fifties and early sixties. There was only one, a Madame DeJacques, straight out of France, whom I liked and remember. She stood with her hands under her armpits in a buttoned light blue cardigan, her swaying breasts held in by a full slip. She demanded that we know her language. We memorized Guy de Maupassant. I learned the words, but I did not get the accent or the pronunciation. My Brooklyn accent seemed to become stronger in French. Every time I spoke her language, Madame DeJacques shook her head violently, which swung her long pearl earlobes back and forth, and she pursed her lips. What excited me about Madame was her energy. Her love of French. Her urgency to make us these little savages—this all-girl class from hick town Farmingdale—learn the music, the depth, the beauty of her native language. And if not that, we should at least not sound like complete fools. How did she end

up among us anyway—a live French woman in suburban Farmingdale? I didn't know.

Once she said in French, "Excusez-moi; je dois aller a la toilette," and bolted out the door. I nudged Mary Ellen in front of me. What did she say? Donna, sitting to my right, intercepted my question and answered loudly, "She has to pee." The class giggled. I sat there, slightly amazed. You mean Madam DeJacques had to go to the bathroom? She had human functions. She was so exotic to me that I had trouble imagining her as a regular person. Once in class I accidentally said, "Je suis français." I meant to say "I speak French" not "I am French." But that was too much for her, that I dared express even accidentally that I was French. She had a ruler in her hand. She pushed out her lips as though about to kiss the air, whipped the stick in circles above her head, and charged at me. "You are not French. You are not French," she said in perfect English, breaking the strict rule of only French spoken in this class.

I was quick that morning. "Je sais, je sais!" I yelled out, meaning "I know, I know." She froze near the window, catching herself in midswing and saw what she was up to. The whole class, including Madame, broke down laughing in huge relief. "Natalie," she said in a sweeping staccato, "someday you will come visit me in Paris."

I was delighted, but I knew that was ridiculous. I had the great fortune to live near New York City. My Aunt Rachel told me that after New York, there is no place else to go. My family orbited the Big Apple, driving to the Bronx to Brooklyn— even a few times dipping down to New Jersey. Once or twice heading for the Catskills. Always near, though, rarely actually going into that great celestial island Manhattan. No. No reason to go to Paris; we had New York. I would probably never travel as far as that. It was beyond my imagination. But I was flattered that Madame had invited me to her hometown, and I nodded my head and smiled.

There was another teacher that had an impact, too. Your English teacher, Mr. Clemente. In one class, he turned the lights down and asked the students to listen to the rain, right?

He turned out the lights and he said, "Okay, just listen to the rain." It was my ninth grade class and we had the big windows in this building. It was raining outside. One of those great spring rains that really fill the earth. It blew me away. There was no test on it. There was no report we had to do. We could just sit and listen to the rain. It was a great relief in my life. It really had a very deep effect on me. I took his classes for the next four years.

And then years later, you made contact with him. You asked him if he remembered you.

I called him and I told him I was the person who wrote *Writing Down the Bones.* He said, "Oh, my God. I know that book, but I never knew one of my students had written it." He didn't remember me because he taught thousands of people. But as we continued to talk, he said, "Wait a minute. I do remember you. You were a thin girl with brown hair in the third seat, fourth row." He said, "Why, Natalie, I never knew you cared that much. You never said a word in class." I said, "Yeah. I was very shy and I was a bit unhappy."

What I realized and why I always emphasize it to teachers is, pay attention to the kids that don't give you any trouble, yet are easy to pass by because if they don't give you trouble, they sort of get by. I said that those people are jewels. They're the ones who are dying, and something is happening there. Honor them.

There was one class where you actually had a 99 in the class and had done very well, and you were pretty much ignored.

Yes. Mr. Burke in fifth grade. I was wild about him. Just wild. He taught science, and so I got completely into science. I got a microscope for Hanukkah and a chemistry set for my birthday. He just had no idea all the effort I made. We had a big term paper we were supposed to do on the Midwestern states. He stood at the end when he was giving out the papers, and he announced the kids' names and then their grades. He went, "Carol Heightsman (someone he liked a lot), ah, she got 97 on her paper. This is the highest paper in the class." Then he named some more people. Then he said, "Natalie Goldberg." He looked at my grade and he said, "Oh, you got 99." He gave it to me. That was it. I remember I didn't get a hundred because I put the bibliography in the front of the book, in front of the report, instead of the back. I didn't know that. So I got a point off. I just wasn't noticed. I was very quiet and shy and disappearing, I guess. But in my heart, I was taking in everything. I think that's true of most kids. They take in very deeply, although they seem faded out. We end up giving attention to the kids who are acting out because they're a pain in the neck. I think people drift forever.

I think of the word inspiration, *and it comes from the word* inspirare *in Latin, "to breathe," and* spiritus *or* spirit, *so we are bringing the spirit forth in some way. That's a beautiful way to look at writing.*

Allan Ginsberg pointed out to me that if you read a good poet aloud, you become high because you're taking on his or her breath at the moment of inspiration. That's ultimately the only thing that can be carried on, which is interesting, because the breath stops when you die, but it's passed on in literature. Understanding it as lineage means that writing and literature is a spiritual practice, and it's passed on.

That's a beautiful way of looking at it. Don't think. Not thinking.

It's really the same thing I said before. "Don't think" means don't go into second and third thoughts. Just stay at the level of first thought. When your thought arises, grab it.

I remember something Krishnamurti used to say. That thinking is the problem. You have to go beyond thinking to another place of knowing.

Yes, or underneath thinking. Usually we think to cover up. Don't worry about the rules of grammar; you can look things up in a dictionary afterwards. Just get down the raw mind. After that, it's simple. Now they have computers where they even correct your spelling. No, don't worry about that.

Do you use a computer?

No, I don't, I do everything by hand. I do that so I can sit in cafes and write. I have mobility. I could sit under a tree. I do give my notebook to my typist. I did have a computer, and I sold it. For the two thousand dollars, I could get four manuscripts typed up. Four manuscripts would last at least eight years. It's so nice because then I have a relationship. You know how lonely being a writer is. I have my typist, who's my friend, who types up my work and then corrects it. I don't have to sit inside and hurt my back. I've given someone a job.

I was projecting that maybe there's some difference between writing with your hand and using a keyboard. Is that something that you found?

Yes, there is a difference. It's a slightly different physical activity, so a slightly different mind comes out. Not better or worse, just a little different, that's all. I like handwriting because it's physical. The handwriting is connected to my arm and my shoulder and my heart. More than anything, it's so I can have mobility. I don't have to stay home. I do all my writing in cafes. I have certain ones where all my books are written.

Yes, it's obvious from reading Wild Mind *that you do like to write in cafes. And why is that? Why do you like cafes?*

First of all, I get out of the house because I daydream. I'm an incredible daydreamer. I drift off in the house, then I make phone calls and, you know, you could find a million reasons not to write. When I get to a cafe, I just have to concentrate because there's a lot of activity around me. Somehow that activity allows me to concentrate deeper. I don't know. I just like that it's a little social. People are around me. I know the waitresses. It's just nice to get out. I meet friends in the cafes to write with. I have dates with people.

There's something you were sharing that you wrote in Wild Mind *about Paris and the cafes in Paris. How it's okay there to sit with a cup of coffee from 9:00 A.M. to 3:00 P.M.*

Yes. It amazes me that in *Writing Down the Bones,* the cafe chapter was everyone's favorite chapter. In Europe, it's no big deal. Everybody writes in cafes. It was an absolute phenomenon here when I wrote that chapter. People would write me that they were scared the first time they went to a cafe. Nobody in America really cares one way or the other, just as long as you're not taking up rush hour when they're making money.

Do you think there's a different sense of writers and writing in Europe than there is in America?

Yes. I think it's much more honored, and it's not considered a growth thing. For instance, a lot of countries wanted to buy *Bones* and then decided not to. They said it's an American phenomenon, because they said there's no such thing. We don't have a lot of writing workshops or books on writing. I think it's considered a high art form in Europe. That you can't pass it on, or you have to know someone to get it passed on. Or you just have to do it; or that old, terrible idea that you have to be hit by a god like lightning. You know you can do it and nobody else knows how. Also, the idea you can't learn to write, which I don't agree with, but they are very clear. It's not that they don't have workshops and stuff. Although Italy took *Bones* and translated it, interestingly enough—the only one. Although I get lots of letters from people in Europe asking how they can get the book. So I have a feeling that if they published it in Europe, it would be gobbled up. There are a lot of secret writers there, too, who don't know how to begin.

What about writing as therapy?

People do it that way. Writing practice is not that. Writing practice burns through to the bottom of your mind, so it might be therapeutic. It's always therapeutic to know who you are, but ultimately when you write, what you find out is that you're no one. You don't exist, and things change all the time.

Would you say you write in notebooks every day?

Yes.

You don't call them journals. Is there a difference between writing in notebooks and writing in a journal?

Yes, for me there is. I always thought of journals as a fascination with emotions and feelings and memories and stuff. Getting almost lost in that. Whereas writing practice uses those things but uses them to burn through. To go to the place where none of it exists. Writing practice knows that the other side of a word is no word. The other side of a life is no life. That it's empty.

That everything has its opposite.

Yes, that finally what you want to do in writing practice is get out of the way. Where writing does writing, and Natalie is gone.

Going back to the rules, one of them is that you're free to write the worst junk in the world.

People go wild over that one. Some people practically break down weeping when I say that one in workshops. It gives you tremendous freedom. I don't know why it is, but we don't give ourselves space to practice with writing. Now everybody knows that with a great tennis player or a football team, that when we see a game on television, they've practiced for many, many hours. You have to practice in writing, too, and be free to write just tremendous junk in order to write something good.

One of the things that struck me about what you wrote is that you said you can throw away the good stuff, too. It'll come again. I was struck by that.

It just keeps coming. People say, "Oh well, do you save all of your notebooks?" I throw them out. They take up room. I will have written much better now than what I wrote ten years ago. If it was worth it, it'll come through me again. You can't hold on to anything.

I just had a twinge when you said that you throw all your notebooks away. I was thinking what if Thomas Merton had done that. We wouldn't have the benefit of all those wonderful journals.

Believe me, mine are mostly garbage.

So you critique yourself?

Oh, that's interesting that you say that. When I say, "Believe me, most of it is garbage," I'm not being critical of myself. I'm just saying the truth. It's different. It's not good or bad.

That's a good point. You're not taking it personally, in other words.

That's right. I'm not taking it personally. Sometimes in my writing groups, I write with everybody, and people say, "Why, your stuff is just like ours." I say, of course, I have the same human mind. The difference between me and my students is that usually I don't care. I'm not attached to it being good or bad.

Most of us take our self-criticisms very personally. It's nice to see someone who doesn't. How do your workshops go? How many people do you have at a workshop, typically?

I'm trying it differently this year. If you come to study with me for a week in Taos where I don't have to travel, I usually take 50 people. We just write and practice every day for five days. When I travel, I'm doing four or five workshops around the country this year. I'm limiting them to a day or two. I tell the organizers that they can do as many people as they want. In a one-day workshop, you really get the stuff. When you're done with me, I've given it to you. The problem is you've got to continue. That's true at a five-day and a year workshop. When it's done, will you continue. That's all that matters.

I've often wondered, because I get all these wonderful fan letters, after they read *Bones,* will they continue? Five years later, are people still writing? That's all it is. Will you continue under all circumstances? If it's not writing, I tell my students to commit yourself to something. Because what happens, especially somehow in Santa Fe, they drift. They're taking a writing workshop with me, and they think they'll become a writer. If it doesn't work, the next week they're getting rolfed. Every week it's something else. I tell them to commit to something, even if it's a marriage. Stay in something under all circumstances.

What are some of the things you've learned from teaching? I know you teach kids and have taught adults. Tell us about some of the lessons you've learned. What have the kids taught you?

Oh, they've taught me tremendous honesty, because they pick up if you aren't telling the truth. They expect you to tell the truth. They've taught me to be spontaneous. To trust in myself. Also, they like repetition, which sounds odd because sometimes you went crazy in school. You repeated so much, but there's a tremendous comfort in going over something. I've slowed down so that I make sure that everyone is with me. It's a great act of compassion not to leave anyone out. Sometimes when I teach adults now, I'll suddenly look at them and say, "You all look like fourth graders." They all nod. Everybody's dying to learn things. What you need to do is slow down and explain it. That's what compassion is. So actually my teaching has fed my writing. I didn't have to slow down and explain everything, but out of my compassion for my readers, I did. Because I wanted them to come along with me. So that teaching really intertwined with my writing and has taught me a lot. Also, I try out stories. I exaggerate stories. I develop them. I learn what they laugh at. Then I get them to laugh more. If I say it a certain way or put a few more details in, I practice with them.

What's the difference for you between writing nonfiction, which you've written up to now in these three books that you've published, and writing fiction?

Fiction is the hardest thing I have ever done. I've done a hundred-day training period in Zen. Writing a novel is harder. What I understand about fiction now is that it's like going under water with no marks for a long time. You're going under to a deep dream and staying there for a long time. Whereas nonfiction is partly a dream, and partially you make it up. What's the truth, anyway, but you have some markers. Like yes, I really did meet Katagiri Roshi. Maybe the relationship with him is a lot from my reality, but at least there are markers. He lived on Lake Calhoun. You know, I have some markers. So it's much more comforting to write nonfiction. Fiction is completely being out of control. I've been working on and off on the book *Banana Rose* for seven-and-a-half years. About 16 months ago, I just suddenly realized what it was about. It wasn't about anything I thought it was about. It was about some deep stuff in my own psyche. Even though it tells a story, the underwater thing was really me working out something big for my psyche.

I'm reminded of a book by Deena Metzger, Writing for Your Life, *which is about using writing as a tool to discover the deeper self. Writing is a tool for doing that. If we follow it deep enough, it'll take us into ourselves in ways that we didn't really expect.*

We don't know who we are. That's why it was so astounding for me to study with Katagiri. This was a human being who knew who he was and had a very deep understanding of what it meant to be a human being. Although he didn't come from this culture, I could go to him with anything, and he could listen and hear it.

What were some of the examples of that, visibly from your perspective, as to why you felt he was a human being, as you say?

Katagiri was quite traditional, actually, a very traditional Japanese man, and then he came to America and had to deal with lesbians and gay people. Just people breaking up marriages and everything. My friend at the Minnesota Zen center lived in Massachusetts and wanted to move to Minnesota to be with Katagiri. She talked to him about it because it was a big move for her. She built a big house in Massachusetts. Then she said, "Listen, I don't know how you feel about this. I don't know if it's okay or what you think, but I've been married for 20 years to a woman. I don't know if you think it's bad." He paused and he said, "It's neither good nor bad. What's her name?"

He came from a very deep place to deal with things on that level. On my first retreat I did with him, you get really high from it. I went to him at the end of it and I said, "Roshi, I feel like I'm on LSD." He said, "Pay no attention to that. That tosses you away. Continue to bow, drink tea, and watch your breath." So the things we thought were so outrageous and something to fight for in our culture came from a place underneath all that. So those are just two examples.

Tell us about your novel Banana Rose.

I began it two weeks after I finished *Writing Down the Bones*. It was going to be autobiographical. I worked on it for three-and-a-half years. Dragged myself through it. It was really hard. I finished it, and it was 550 pages. I couldn't shut up. I knew nothing about novels. I just dove in, and that's usually how I do things. I'll figure it out in the midst of doing it. I left it for nine months after I finished it, and then I got up the nerve to ask three very good friends who are great novelists to read it and comment. One of the novelists read it and said there's no plot. It's plotless. Now nine months earlier, I would have burst out crying, but I just burst out laughing. I said to her, "What is a plot, anyway?" It took me all that time to be willing to ask. If I'd asked earlier, I wouldn't have gotten it when she told me what it was. So just a month ago, I started rewriting it. So that's a year and a half after I finished it. I went through one revision and cut out 200 pages. I'm going to do another revision, and then I'll send it out again.

Is it still autobiographical?

Yes, but you know what I've learned is that the more you work on something, the more your past disappears. It's just something that you've carried around in your head. If you turn around, the past is no place but in your head. What I've realized was that it was something I was making up all along, anyway.

The idea of the space that a novel affords is that it's different from writing nonfiction, isn't it?

It's completely different. You become friends with these characters. Nell Schwartz, whose alias, Banana Rose, was my darling. You know I love Nell more than anybody around, unfortunately. When the novel was done, I really crashed. Here was my best friend, and she didn't exist. Yes, it's very different. I think a novel is definitely the hardest thing I've ever done. It really breaks your back. Nobody tells you that ahead of time. When I was halfway through it, I was sitting with friends who've written many novels, and I said, "Why didn't you tell me?" They didn't say a word. Their faces took on these agonized expressions, and they just shook their head like, Could we have told you? One of them spent eight years on her novel.

It sounds like it's almost compulsive in some way.

No. Compulsive isn't the word. It hurts.

It's like going into your own pain. Into your own shadow.

I guess so. I study writing practice and process, and I don't really understand the depth of why it hurts. Even when the writing is good and it goes really well, you're stripping yourself raw. I feel like I'm not really here. I don't think people talk enough about that part. Luckily I have friends like my friend Kate Green, who's one of my best writing friends. When I was finishing *Banana Rose,* I called her. I said, "Kate, I don't understand it. I'm pissed off all the time. I'm really angry." She said, "Of course. You're finishing a novel." I said, "What does that have to do with it?" She said, "I don't know, but I'm always angry when I'm finishing a novel."

When I thought about it, the energy of anger is also an energy of change pushing me through. It's almost like giving birth. Also, there was the anger that I'd sacrificed my life for this book. You know what my friend Marion says: "Use by the muse."

Anger could also be fear. It could be fear of the what lays beyond this. This is kind of a known in some ways.

Yes. Also that you've given everything, and it's over. It's sort of like a divorce or a death. It can give you the truth of what is, and sometimes we don't want to know that. You can't hold on to anything. Everything changes, and it's all impermanent.

I can hear your Buddhism coming in there with your writing perspective. The process that you're teaching in your workshops, are you able to convey this kind of detachment to your students? Is your intensity from your approach to writing transferable to others?

When you get into writing practices, once it starts moving and you write with a group, you pick up on the group energy. You just can't stop writing. The stuff pours out of you. Topic: french fries. Oh God, what am I going to write about french fries? Then you start going into it. Your memories of your grandmother, and this and that, you know. You start entering your own life. It's very wild and very exciting.

A number of exercises you have in the book begin with certain things such as, "I'm thinking" or "I remember." These are short ten-minutes bursts that you just go with.

I do those exercises regularly. It doesn't really matter what you start with or what the topic is. It's just an entry into your own mind. Once you start entering, your own stuff comes up and you don't know what it'll be.

One of the terms in the book that you used is monkey mind. *What's monkey mind?*

Monkey mind is actually a Buddhist term. It's that part that's always distracted, never present. It's always trying to create trouble or get its nose stuck in something. It's just never satisfied. It doesn't allow us to be where we are.

How does nature affect your writing?

Probably not very much. I'm not very good at writing about nature. I love nature. I live in Taos, which is all about the land. But as far as my writing, that's a good question. No one's ever asked me that. I have nothing to say about nature. It is just there. I seem to write more about cafes and drinking coffee, which actually I don't drink, but I like the idea of drinking coffee. Nature affects my life more than my writing, except that it brings me to the big place.

I made a pilgrimage once to the gravesite of D. H. Lawrence outside of Taos. You've spent time there.

Yes, his ashes are there. Actually, it's the place I do workshops in Taos. He used to live there at the Mable Dodge House. He painted the bathroom windows at the Mable Dodge House. Yes, he lived in Taos, and there's a Lafonda Hotel on the plaza that has his old porn paintings. They aren't very erotic for now, but they have them. You can pay a dollar and go into someone's office and see them.

Do you refer to other writers in your workshops?

Writing, as you said, is a lineage, and you pass it on, so yes, definitely.

What writers would you set up as models?

Recently I've used Hemingway a lot. I've been reading Paul Zweig. A book of memoirs called *Departures: Fierce Attachments,* by Vivian Gorneck, is quite a wonderful book. Also Jean Reese, who's an English writer.

Do you read a lot of other writers?

Yes, of course. I wouldn't be so arrogant to think I know everything.

Do you learn things from reading other writers?

Of course. What you do when you read a book by a writer is you're studying their mind and taking on their way of seeing. Sometimes I'll read only one writer for a year. I'll read a book over and over until I get that mind inside me, because that's what it is. It's passing on. It's like an apprenticeship. That's how you learn to write.

You did that with Hemingway, didn't you?

Yes, I guess I did. I've certainly read him a lot. You know what I do? I'll read the same passage that I'll fall in love with in every workshop. Not so much for my students, but for me. So that gets imprinted.

And you followed some of his pathways in Europe.

Yes. I went to his cafes in Paris and wrote in all of them.

*I'm reminded of Rupert Sheldrake's theory of morphic reso-
nance and the morphogenetic fields of energy that are left by the
kinds of things that take place in certain places. In Paris you can
feel that there's a morphogenetic field of energy that's different
from other places. What about Taos, New Mexico?*

I love Taos. It's my heart's home. I don't get much writing
done there. I daydream a lot. I have a house on a mesa that's
made by Michael Reynolds, who does buildings, completely
solar buildings, using recycled materials—beer cans and tires—
and I have photovoltaic electricity, which means all of my electricity comes from the sun. But I mostly daydream up there.
People think, *Oh, it's a great place to write, but it's too isolated
for me.* Taos is really my heart's home. I was a hippie there in the
early seventies. Then I left for seven years, and I could never get
over it. So, finally I just moved back.

And so you go down into town to write.

I go to Santa Fe. There's a place in Santa Fe where I write and
I walk along the streets. Then I return to Taos and daydream.

*I'd like to go back to writing as a spiritual practice and
explore that a little more. What does that mean?*

I think it's the thing that I've taken on—to find out what it
means to be a human being and to be alive on the earth. I use
writing practice as a way to penetrate my life and to wake up.
That's pretty much what it means for me.

*So through the process of writing, you're able to reflect back
to yourself what's going on?*

Yes, and through the process of writing, I'm able to step into a bigger world. To really go into my own wild mind. Beyond my ego.

We usually think of wildness as something outside of accepted normality. Something not to be treasured or pursued. In fact, I think there's a lot of fear around wildness. I think we have drummed into us early on as children the fear of wild things. You'd better watch out—it's wild out there, you know. What about that?

First of all, we all are incredibly wild and outrageous , as if we just stepped out of that little place in us I call monkey mind that wants to control everything. For instance, when I was in Minnesota, everybody would make these gorgeous little gardens in the summer with petunias and columbine. Then we would long to be in the woods where everything was seemingly disorderly, but we felt peaceful. So we have a longing to come back to that place where things are not logical, but yet we really belong there. We can settle in there. The truth is that life is very wild, very wild. We have no idea about anything, but we think we do. The earthquake is a great example. We think we all know what we are doing, and then the very earth under your feet falls apart. Before that, you always probably could say, "Well, at least I know the earth is below my feet." Well, no, you don't know that even. So Wild Mind writing practice brings you into that place of wild mind—that huge place where we all are interconnected and interpenetrated. There's no separation.

It was Thoreau who said, "In wildness is the preservation of the world." And in some ways—it's probably part of the reason why we have environmental problems today—we've lost that sense of wildness.

We're trying to control everything, and finally we think we're going to control death. You know, we try to control the atom. The smallest particle that we're made up of, and look at what we've done with it. You know it's backfired on us. We've created the atom bomb. Yes, I think that if we could live with our own wildness, we won't have to control everything outside ourselves. I think Robert Bly talks about that a lot, doesn't he? About the wild man, or coming back to that.

Recovering the wild man. Yes, inside, and I assume there's a wild woman as well.

Oh, yes, there definitely is.

I've met her a few times. I've met wild man a few times. I definitely have met the wild woman, so they're both around.

And the wild earth and just about every wild animal. Everything is wild, big, alive, and full of energy.

Do you start with a title? Do you clearly have a title for a book before you start?

Yes, I usually have a title that comes to me.

Some writers don't have a title. They just get into writing, and then the title comes later.

I've always known the title. Like *Banana Rose,* the novel. I turned a corner in Santa Fe in my car and thought of Banana Rose. When I thought of that, I knew I could write the book. It's almost like if I can get the title, I can write the book.

Does traveling influence your writing?

I love to travel. I was traveling a lot for workshops, and it burned me out. Now I travel just to travel. It's important to me. Traveling informs my writing, and it stimulates me. I write while I travel. I get a lot of work done then. So it doesn't keep me back.

There's something about traveling that does broaden one's horizons.

Traveling makes me alive again. I notice what's in front of my nose—which is what the ideal is—to be able to do that at home. It's traveling that kind of wakes me up.

I think part of the magic of traveling is leaving home and being in a place that's not a comfort zone for us. So it kind of creates a composting process that may not exist at home. We're a little more alert when we travel.

Some people don't like to travel. William Carlos Williams was born in, and died in, Rutherford, New Jersey, and he wrote some pretty good poems. I think it matters who you are, too. I feel bad if I leave out everything in my writing. I like to be able to throw in Spain or other countries or other worlds, even if it's just Kansas City. I like to include everything, eventually.

🜂   🜂   🜂

EPILOGUE

"If you go all the way with the writing, it'll take you every place Zen does. Anything you commit yourself to completely, you'll have to face." Just as Katagiri Roshi told Natalie Goldberg to use writing as her spiritual practice, his admonition applies to all forms of creative expression. Perseverance. Persistence. Patience. Three words whose meaning requires a tenacity of spirit. A longing. A capacity to stick to it, whatever it is, no matter what. This is the key. If there is a secret to manifesting creativity, this is it. Whatever it is we commit our creative energy to totally without equivocation will lead us on an amazing journey. Set aside a specific time each day to explore and express your creativity. Do not be distracted. Honor your deeper self. Pursue your passion and live your dream.

CHAPTER THREE
❧ ❧ ❧

Writing: The Gateway to the Inner World

Deena Metzger, with Michael Toms

PROLOGUE

*C*reativity is a natural birthright for all of us. However, many
of us choose not to embrace this capacity out of fear. Yet it is
a gift and a sacred trust asking us to accept it, nurture it, develop it, and pass it on. Everyone has a writer within. This inner
writer is a guide to amazing worlds—fantastic regions where
anything is possible. In harsh landscapes, we can count our lim-
itations and go beyond them to experience the joy of creation.
Writing brings about the wonder of self-knowledge and the ability to heal what is fragmented, injured, or suppressed within us.

Novelist, poet, playwright, and essayist Deena Metzger has
worked over the past two decades as a psychotherapist and healer in private practice. She's lectured and presented workshops on
a variety of topics, including the creative process, theater, ecolo-

gy, cancer, spirituality, women's studies, world peace, and disar-mament. She's the author of several collections of poetry, includ-ing The Woman Who Slept with Men to Take the War Out of Them; Looking for the Faces of God; *and* A Sabbath Among the Ruins; *a novel called* What Dinah Thought; *and* Writing for Your Life: Discovering the Story of Your Life's Journey.

🔥 🔥 🔥

MICHAEL TOMS: *Deena, can you tell us your thoughts on writ-ing as a gateway to the inner world?*

DEENA METZGER: I think we should start with the inner worlds. Actually, while you were out of the country, they changed the subtitle of the book, which is now called *A Guide and Companion to the Inner Worlds.* We changed it because I wanted people to realize the dimensions of the cosmos that's out there. Sometimes our own lives seem small because they're not set within that larger dimension. It was my hope with this book that those worlds would open up to people.

What about the natural fear that we have about sitting down with pen and paper? There's a natural tendency to shy away from wanting to do that.

Well, whenever I teach writing and someone says, "I'm real-ly afraid," that's when I get excited. I think, *Good! We're afraid of writing because we fear that we will define ourselves.* I don't mean limit, but define ourselves in the sense of knowing or rec-ognizing ourselves through what we set down. We're also afraid that we won't say "it" well enough. That in setting something down we will limit ourselves. Or that we'll say something that is not quite as relevant as we would like it to be. I think that in this

culture, we are so disconnected from the imagination and creativity that we have great fears that we won't be able to get there,
and fears that we will. I think that we have to just be aware of the
fear and see if we can change it into excitement.

*Why do you think we're so disconnected from imagination
and creativity?*

Because imagination and creativity have to do with possibility. They have to do with multiplicity and diversity. We live
increasingly in a mono culture in which our thoughts, our behaviors, the way we dress, what we think, what we see, how we
behave—all of that is seriously prescribed and limited. If someone enters into the other world of the imagination, that person is
almost by definition a rebel in that moment. We don't like rebels
in this culture. We have the illusion of freedom, but I think it's a
serious illusion.

*So actually, writing to go into those inner worlds is a
rebellion?*

I think it's a rebellion. I think it's a revolutionary act because
in that act, one is, as I say in the book, constructing a self. To be
a real human being in this society is difficult and rare and very
precious. Remember in one of Carlos Castaneda's early books,
Don Juan said that a real human being was like a luminous egg.
He was looking within. He was able to see the shining quality of
the human being that was too often clothed and hidden. Well,
writing is perhaps a way of becoming a luminous egg.

*So what's a good place to start writing? I mean, one
wouldn't necessarily start writing a novel, but how about keeping
a journal?*

You start with a journal. You start with your story. I think every life is a story and that we are living out these stories for our entire life each day. You can start anywhere. You can start with something you saw today. One of the exercises in the book is: Things you didn't see today. By that I mean things that happened, things that you saw only out of the corner of your eye, that you didn't have the time to stop and pay attention to. You can start there. What was it that you didn't pay attention to? Start with a dream. If you don't dream, you can make up a dream. You can really start anywhere. That's the point of it. The point is to jump in.

Bringing in dreams reminds me of the dream police. Tell us about the dream police.

That's one of my favorite exercises, and it goes something like this: Imagine that the dream police are coming to your house. You suddenly get the alarm—they're coming. You have only 20 minutes, and everything that you don't record within that time will be erased. So then the task is to write down everything that you care about, everything that matters. You will quickly see that the substance of your life is so much more complex than you would think because, for example, if you don't write down history, history will go. If you don't write down the dark, you'll live in a saccharin and superficial world. When you do this exercise, you just can't write down music. What music? Which composer? Which musician?

You can't just write down women. You have to write down which women.

Which women—I'm afraid you do—and also which memories. Which animals. Which places that you visited. Everything.

So specificity is important.

Specificity is the core of writing. You quickly learn that if you just write things generally, it doesn't have any excitement or magic to it. You've got to name names.

So you can't just write things.

No. Well, I suppose you could do some kind of poem that reads: *things things things things things things.* But after a while, you want to say which things, which bird. That one over there with the blue wing going toward the moon.

Once there was a woman in my class who did that dream-police exercise. She, fortunately, read last. After everyone else had listed their animals, the lake, the birds, the historical moments, the books, the people in their lives, everything that really mattered to them in particular, she listed "books, Thrifty, drug store, Safeway, her credit cards, the bank," etc. She sort of saved the mundane world for us. However, the life that she was going to live was going to be terrible because there was nothing in it but institutions.

It sounds like it's not just a writing exercise, but also an exercise in understanding what our attachments are, what we can let go of.

Because in that moment you have to make a choice. You do let go of things. There's a story that's told in Barbara Meyerhoff's collection, *Last Talks and Tales.* It's the story of a man who actually spent a great deal of time underground during World War II. He was a young boy, and his mother told him that the armies would surely come and he would have to be ready. He had to put the things that he cared about in a shoe box. That was all that he would be able to take with him. So he put his comb and a pair of socks and gloves and scarf and clean underwear and all that stuff into one shoe box. Then he looked at it, and it was very dissatisfying to him. So he took another shoe box and into that one he put his journal, his mementos, photographs, letters he had received, a rock from the place he came from, and some pressed leaves and flowers.

Then one day he did come home from school and his mother said, "Now, run!" and he picked up a shoe box and he ran with it. When they got to their destination and they were about to get on the train that was going to take them to who knows what forsaken place, he opened the shoe box. He said, "Oh, my God, I took the wrong shoe box. How am I going to live without those other things?"

Well, the wonderful thing about this story is that every time Barbara Meyerhoff, who was an anthropologist, told this story, it was a different shoe box that he had taken. So the question is: "How was he going to live without his underwear, and how was he going to live without his letters?" At each time in our life, we have to make a choice. Sometimes we need the comb, and sometimes we need the stone.

It's interesting how so often things define who we are. Or what we do defines who we are. Would you agree that it's important sometimes to separate oneself from one's role? For example, traveling to a different place is a way to remove yourself from your normal environment. It's a way to open yourself to new experiences and new possibilities.

Well, I know you were just in Bali. So you have the experience of dropping the outer world. When you do that, then two things happen: One, I suspect you really saw Bali in a way that you might not have if you had to see it through the glaze of this life here. But the other is that I suspect you really came to know yourself, because there's something raw and fresh about who we are when we drop these impediments. I always hoped that that young boy took the shoe box with the letters in it. Even if he didn't know how, it would help him survive. I deeply believe that these mementos of spirit would nurture him ultimately.

Something you wrote that was intriguing was: "When I don't find time to write, I'm aware that I'm not finding time for myself."

The way I treat my writing is the way I treat myself. It was one of those profound understandings. It's as if my writing and my psyche are one. That the writing is the deepest, most precious part of myself. When I ignore it, I'm just not paying attention. Then I'm living a conventional life, and living it by rote, but I'm not attending what we call *self* in that deep way.

So writing is an experience for you that is deeply connected to your innermost essence.

I can almost feel it. It's as if that's the time when I can feel myself. There are times when words come, and they have a palpability to them. I hate to use this word but they really do have a *vibration*. When they come out of my body, they come out with a certain hum or sound. That hum or sound has meaning attached to it—not because the words connote something, but because they are something in and of themselves. At the same time, they feel like myself. It's as if I am touching this being that I don't get to hold in my hands otherwise. Maybe that's why writers often like to write at dawn or late at night when things are very quiet; there's something magical about those times. Magical about the light. Magical about the stillness. We look for a pristine setting in which we can encounter ourselves. Of course, as I was saying this, I was thinking about all the writers I know who like to write at cafes and in New York and on the subway. That's a whole other scene, but there is some way in which one comes alive, enacting oneself in that open moment. You know what I mean?

Yes. It's almost like a mystical experience in some way.

Yes, mystical. Very sensual. Very sensory. You can touch the spirit or the soul in those moments.

There was an experience that I had in Bali that I was reminded of as you were talking. There was this ancient Balinese village over a thousand years old where they are famous for double-ikat weaving. Where they produce beautiful tapestries and weavings with this double ikat. Don't ask me to explain it, but it's very intricate, very involved, and it takes a very long time. So for a very small piece of cloth three feet long, maybe a foot wide, it might take six months to make.

I had this question: Why would anyone spend six months weaving this piece of cloth? I mean, it's expensive by Balinese standards. They sell it to tourists and visitors and so forth, and compared to other Balinese cloths, it's relatively expensive. If you figure the time it requires, the labor works out to maybe ten cents an hour. So it's not being done for the money. So I found myself in this village where they did this work. I was talking to a Balinese man who had some command of English, and I realized as he was talking and explaining this piece of cloth, that to them the whole process of doing this was very much a part of their spiritual practice. It was like a prayer. The aspect of whether it was sold for how much didn't matter. It was the prayer of doing it. It was like this realization of the idea of being one with your work and what that really is about.

We hear the words, but we don't really know what they mean. It's like, why would someone sit on a cushion for an hour a day or 20 minutes or weeks at a time. We don't really understand that. I didn't know what you were going to say, but when you said "prayer," I was so glad you said that. Because prayer always seems so much more active to me than meditation. It has a longing to it. A reaching out, as if in the act of prayer I'm trying to bring my being toward the deity. Just trying to get it a little closer, and because I feel so much awe for the divine, I have to do it as well as I can. It can take a very long time. I mean, like a lifetime, right?

In a sense, what else does one want to do? Writing has that same quality for me. When a novel comes to me, it often comes like something knocking at the door. I have to decide if I'm going to open that door because it could take ten years. I'm writing a novel now, and I don't know if I'm going to finish it in February, as I hope, or if it will take me another five years. There's no way of rushing it. In a way, I also don't want to finish it because I'm so glad to be with it. Such writing is sometimes like a really fine marriage. You want to spend as much time as you can with this being, with this piece of work. You know that you're going to grow from the connection. That I'm not the writing, I'm separate from it, and it's separate from me, but something happens when the two of us come together.

What about writing what you don't know?

You must always write what you don't know. It's very boring to write what you do know. That's like being a secretary. The whole task is to go into the unknown. I guess that's what I wanted to do in this book—guide people into the unexplored territory. Sort of an odd thing, because that means then that I'm guiding them someplace that I don't know either. But in a funny way, I think I do know the unknown. I think that's my territory. Writing what you don't know is the equivalent of, let's say, painting something. If you write what you know, it's like illustrating a book. You know it. But you start writing, and one thing leads to another, and your task is simply to follow it because the creative unconscious is so much wiser than we are. That's really the point. The mind, the rational mind, the will, the ego, those parts of ourselves that have to negotiate in the daily life—they don't know everything. There are other parts of us, though, that have access to everything.

It's something like what Jung meant by the *collective unconscious*. Only in my mind, it not only takes in the past and all of human knowledge, I think it takes in the future. I think it takes in other worlds. I think it takes in the language of trees and animals. What's important about that is that the imagination is a real place. We simply have to learn how to enter into it.

What about retreats for writing?

A retreat is anything we do to get away from what distracts us. I was thinking recently about fascism, which I see rising up everywhere in the world. Fascism is the totalitarian imposition upon a self or a psyche of a certain and particular way of being. One of the ways that I think that we are succumbing to fascism is through distraction, through all the tasks—the mindless and useless tasks—that we have to do in order to survive in the world and to accommodate the speed-up of life. So if we are to contact this very delicate and fragile but luminous part of ourselves, we have to create some kind of world, some kind of wall around our lives, so that we can go inside.

So I regularly try to get away for a few weeks, or with any luck, for a month or two, so that the world can fall away the way you were describing when you went to Bali. Then I can really begin to write what needs to be written. Now sometimes, of course, one can't get away, and in this culture it becomes more and more impossible for us to find that kind of time. So then the question is: "How can you create a retreat within an hour?" Some of this resembles the ways of contemplative practice, of meditation. One enters a special room, lights a candle, does a ritual that tells the psyche that this is sacred space, and then that little moment comes be a retreat. Turn the phones off. Find a view, to sit with a pad and look at a tree. In the city or in the woods, if you're looking at a tree, if you're really letting yourself look at it, that can be a moment of retreat.

I want to ask you about the guide. Tell us about the process of guide.

When we're going into the unknown, it's nice to have someone take us. Since the only one that can take us in is someone that comes from that territory, it's a very special being that we need to affiliate ourselves with. Many years ago when I was teaching at California Institute for the Arts, I became aware of the fragility of my students. This was in the seventies; it seemed to be a dangerous time. A lot of people were working with drugs. They were going into inner worlds, but they really didn't know how to contain or control their experience. It occurred to me that one could do a meditation within which one could connect with an inner figure. Now I do not wish to say whether this is someone from inside ourselves or someone from another world or a spirit. We don't know.

Or, God help us, the word channel.

Yes. I suppose so. So what I did was design a meditation. It's actually quite common now. Probably many of you people who are reading this have done such a meditation. One, for example, takes a walk—well, first one quiets down—that's the important thing—and then walks to a place, and over a period of time of asking for guide to appear, comes to some meeting. The first time that I did this, I was very arrogant. I had designed the guide meditation for my students, thinking that I already had a guide. In my imagination, I felt very connected with Ariadne, who had held the thread for Theseus to enter the labyrinth. That seemed like a very useful image, one who holds the thread, and so I was quite content to use this figure as an inner guide.

But after my students came back with some very interesting and unexpected guides, I decided to do the exercise myself. I sat down, and I did all the steps that I had advised them to do, and I heard what seemed to me a clanking in my mind. So, as instructed, I said, "Who are you?" The voice said, "Athena." I said, "Athena?" I was outraged. I'd never thought about Athena. I didn't like Athena. But I remembered that I had instructed my students that they had to accept whoever came. After all, I was talking to a god. I thought I'd better be polite. You don't know what danger you're going to get into if you're sassy and disrespectful.

So I confessed, "You know, I've never really thought about you." She said, "I've never been mothered." This was an astonishing idea to me. Though I knew the myth of Athena and that she was born out of Zeus's head, I had never thought about the corollary, which was that this meant that she did not have a mother. I was also aware of what it meant for women at that time to feel unmothered in the world. Also, in my own experience, I sometimes felt very much like my mother's mother, I had not had a powerful feminine maternal influence.

Also, I was involved at that particular time in a First Amendment academic freedom case. Athena said to me, "Look at this. Look at my neck. Look at the armor I'm wearing. Look at how it chafes me." Then I was again aware that Athena was a warrior and that she was suffering from this.

The third thing she said was it had been considered laughable that Athena should compete in a contest of beauty with someone like Aphrodite. She said, "You know, even though I am a goddess, no one takes me seriously as a woman." I thought, *Well, this is really one of the conflicts of our time.* This was at the height of feminism. Women were going out in the world, but they had to choose. They could either be considered beautiful, sexual women who would partner with men, or they could to go off and be intellectual, academic, and powerful. But the two had not come together. So what really happened to me is that Athena—an inner voice, some spirit, some intelligence—spoke to me in exceedingly profound ways. I was humbled by this. I began to call upon Athena actively whenever I went into the inner world, when I sat down to write. It was a part of my retreat or meditation.

To this day, when I sit down to write, though it may not be Athena I'm invoking, I quiet myself and call on the spirit to help me across. In part, I do this because I believe that the creative act is one that brings the worlds together. That creativity is an ethical collaboration with the gods. I want to bring beauty, and I want it to bring meaning to the larger world. I want it to be for the world in a way that is spiritually wise. So I need help. I call on it.

And each of us has the capacity to discover our own inner guide?

Absolutely. I mean, the stories that come are really wonderful. I haven't worked with anyone who didn't find a guide, who wasn't surprised by the guide that came. Sometimes the guide doesn't come the first time. We try again. We have to be patient, but I really believe that those who are willing to make the bridge to the other world are met by figures from the other world who also want to make an alliance with us.

I want to ask you about the magic of "once upon a time."

Once upon a time is always now and always forever. Once upon a time is a sacred place and a sacred time in which miracles happen. It's the essence of a fairy tale. It's the essence of story. When we hear it, we become a child. That is, we become innocent. We are ready and able to understand what is mysterious. In once upon a time, the figures from the demiworlds the little spirits, the fairies, the goblins, the elves, the devas—they all come. These fairy tales are very, very wise.

That's another thing that happens in fairy tales. Everything is *very, very* dark. The princess is *very, very* beautiful. The prince is *very, very* sad, etc. We enter into a world in which we understand something of what we really are living. Because we really are all Cinderella. There isn't any one of us who hasn't known what it is to be rejected in that way. What it is to sit in the soot. What it means to be the prince who is wandering. Looking for someone that he danced with fleetingly who then disappeared. I mean, you can hear as you listen to the story the way it speaks our journeys. As we read these tales, we learn very much what the rules of that other world are and how to live in it. In other words, we learn something about one of the worlds that we have a right to live in but don't often encounter.

Or we live in a world that really disdains the irrational and suppresses the invisible world. I mean, we don't recognize the invisible world. It's only if it's visible and rational that we should believe it.

I think, for example, about Hansel and Gretel. Why do we tell our children the story of Hansel and Gretel? Because if they don't know what it means to be lost in the woods, they will not survive this life. I don't mean if they don't know how to use a literal mechanical compass. I mean if they don't know how to negotiate the woods. If they don't know about hunger in a way that the story speaks about hunger. And if they don't know the companionship that they could have with each other, confronted with hunger. The stepmother's hunger, which throws them out. The hunger of the birds who eat the crumbs so that the children lose their way. Then the hunger of the witch who wants to devour them. If we don't know that we might be devoured and how to protect ourselves, we really won't survive. So when these stories are translated into cheerful Disney versions, the wisdom is taken out of them. Now I think that every child who hears the real story identifies with all the characters, but particularly with Hansel and Gretel. Then, as adults, we can go back into that story. We can write it again where we are Gretel or Hansel or the witch, and see where that takes us. What understanding it gives us.

What about writing your own myth?

Well, to write your own myth, you have to really know what myth is. That myth is that larger story that is always looming at the edge of our reality, that lives *us* in a way and that *we* live. When we understand that story, that all of us, for example, have been in the paradise of the garden, and all of us have fallen; when we understand that all of us carry that cross on our backs upon which we all be crucified; that all of us are Psyche, who has not trusted that she was with the God in the dark—therefore, against the gods' instruction, she brought a light, a rational self to the bedroom, to the place where they were intimate and she frightened Eros away—when we understand that those stories are alive in us all the time and that we follow them, then it's as if the story is born in us, and our life is transformed. It is possible to see the stages in a myth, those archetypal moments that repeat themselves. To trace our own story to see where our life coincides with the archetypal story. It's as if the life that we were living, which was being lived in a two-dimensional way, is suddenly miraculously rounded out and three-dimensional.

I remember a moment, for example, when I was "Lost." We have to hear all these words. You know, capital *L* and resonant. A friend of mine, Cory Fisher from the Traveling Jewish Theater, turned to me after hearing me speak. He said, "Oh, I understand you're lost, but you're lost in the desert." A lightbulb went on because I knew about Christ being in the desert and dealing with the temptations of Satan. I knew that the Israelites were wandering in the desert. I knew about Joseph in the desert. I began to see where my life and those myths coincided. It was actually one of the times when a novel came out and gripped me because I became fascinated with the myth of Dinah, who was the daughter of Jacob. Then I understood that I had to write her story. In that novel, Dinah's life and the life of contemporary American women are superimposed. One on the other. To deal with myth is going into another dimension. Maybe it's not going from second to third. Maybe it's going to the fourth or the tenth.

EPILOGUE

The creative process takes us on a journey into who we are, and Deena Metzger invites us to know the story of our life through writing. Writing allows us to open to the mysteries of our imagination with a deep trust that it will lead us to where we need to go. As we discover the depths and richness of our own original story, meaning and purpose emerge, and through them healing makes us whole. The power of story to reveal our innermost truths and enable us to understand the warp and woof of the tapestry of our life lies at the core of the writing process. The act of writing itself leads us on a path into the unknown. One step unfolds into another, and we are led into the mapless territory of the imagination where all things are possible. It is a real place, and it is inside us.

CHAPTER FOUR

The Creative Power of the Moment

Keith Jarrett, with Michael Toms
and fellow interviewer Phil Catalfo

PROLOGUE

Among music lovers everywhere, Keith Jarrett is known as an artist of rare gifts. Over the past quarter-century, he has created music in many different forms: orchestral works, jazz combos, solo compositions—which could be called tone poems—and solo piano improvisations, for which he is perhaps best known. What emerges out of the body of his work is a sensibility that is, at its essence, spiritual. For in his approach to making music, it seems that Keith Jarrett is continually searching for what he calls "the point of entry" into the music—searching to enter the music in order to play it, searching for whatever lies beyond the entrance.

MICHAEL TOMS: *Keith, I'd like to go back to your own origins when you first consciously became aware of music. I wonder if you can recall that for us.*

KEITH JARRETT: I'm not sure it was conscious at all. It was an awareness that music played a large part in my life and was going to continue to. That was when I was quite young—perhaps between three and six. I naturally couldn't have put it into words at the time, but whenever my mother threatened to sell the piano, it became very important to keep it. There was no other major activity that I felt I was responsible for, that I was going to be responsible for continuously. Everything else seemed like something that needed to be done and would be done, but music was a constant.

MICHAEL: *Can you carry the process forward and reflect on how your consciousness became more aware of your music, your motivation with music.*

I just wasn't afraid of what it meant to be responsible for music. I think that's the whole statement. I wasn't afraid of that. So I would turn toward a certain kind of music that I hadn't heard before. I would get what was in that music, and whether I used it or not was something else, but I was not afraid to plumb the depths of sounds. Also, I wasn't afraid to make mistakes with it because I'm sure I was aware that the mistakes were just a part of the whole thing. I couldn't have put it into words then, either, but now I can talk about how important mistakes are.

MICHAEL: *What were your teachers like?*

I must have had an incredible teacher when I was three to even take me on. We were in a small Pennsylvania town.

Obviously, she was willing to do something that probably very few teachers around there would have done. But all I remember of her is the gate at the top of her stairs.

PHIL CATALFO: *Was there a certain point at which your involvement with music went from being an interest, to being, for want of a better word, a "calling"?*

I don't think it was so musical a discovery around the age of, let's say, 19 or 20, that what I had been feeling were not emotions. They were more or less based on laws. So if we were talking of music, I would say there was some sonic reality that if tapped would produce music automatically. Up to that point, I thought, *You improvise and sometimes it's good, but why is it good?* Why is it bad other times? Why do some people who are really messed up play wonderful music, and some people who are ready for anything and capable of moving all over their instrument incapable of making any music out of it? There was a point that had nothing to do with music. It just had to do with the realization that there were people who understood this other than in an emotional way. There was a way of looking at it from many, many ways. That it wasn't expressing an emotion. I think that was very big. I honestly can't remember how I felt before that moment about music. So my other 19 years, I know what I did, and they were facts in my life, but I don't know how I let them be absorbed up to that moment.

PHIL: *I'm interested in the point you just made about this discovery being distinct from emotion—distinct from the emotional power of music. Certainly speaking for myself, when I experience your music, a lot of times I have an emotional experience. Sometimes I think I'm receiving an emotional communication.*

Distinct from emotion the way Emerson means emotion when he says do your own thing, and everyone takes that as an emotional statement, which it isn't. Emerson's complete statement has much more to it, which is that he said do your own thing and I will know you. But in that same essay, he's talking about how there are two ways to go about things following laws that you choose to believe in, and the other way is to do exactly what you know to do at every second or every moment.

Well, when you see someone doing that, you get an emotional quality from that activity and that person. But the person is not emotionally involved only in what he's doing. He is totally involved at that moment. People mistake that often for an emotional involvement, a mystical experience. It looks emotional to someone who's watching. Emotional with a small *e,* let's say. But the mystic would have to say yes, it's emotional, but that's one part, you know. He would probably say it's colorless. So if we speak of emotions as having color, then I would say this was at the point where I realized we're not just painting canvases with color and erasing them and painting another canvas with color. We're trying to find a clarity, and there are people who are aware of this already. That I'm not alone in being out here thinking there's more to this. That was when I was 19. After that point, I had strength to do just about whatever I knew to do. In Emerson's terminology, hopefully.

MICHAEL: *You discovered something that I think a lot of us look for in the sense that it applies to all of life. It's a principle of life, in the sense that searching is not just limited to the arts and music, is it?*

No. In a way, artists are in a worse position in general to have this experience because they are emotionally attached to their tool. Their tool is considered one of expression. Expression is considered emotional. While all those things are true, they aren't the truth. I have experiences often at concerts where the listeners that really were able to listen were not professional listeners or professional musicians. They were people who happened to be in the hall for some reason, who had no idea what I would do or not do. So they had no history bank to use or associative thing to use. They received exactly what happened. They can come backstage sometimes and say this happened here, and I realized this is the same thing again. I'm hearing from a total stranger who isn't at all involved in my discipline, let's say, or my work, that what I'm doing isn't personal emotion at all; it's an objective thing. That they just came back and said this is what that was, wasn't it? So it has something to do with the fact that that experience was gigantic in that respect, but you don't have to play the piano. I play the piano too often.

PHIL: *Too often in what sense?*

Well, I have to say will I do this or won't I do this? If I say I will do it, it's confirmed. There's a contract. So obviously I'm playing the piano much more than I need to play the piano to have this experience. I am very aware of that. So, the very first generation of this state is synthetic, and the rest is natural.

MICHAEL: *Have you discovered other ways to generate the experience outside of playing music?*

I don't like the synthetic generation at all, so that's what I mean about playing too much. It would be better for me to let the experience go when it goes, and come when it comes, and work on it when it's there, and work on its presence when it's not there. I mean, learn as it's coming. But when I have what you might call a forced experience, which I have to have, it is as natural as the others, but the very beginning has to be generated somehow. Actually, that's even more interesting in some respects than the experience itself. That's something I discovered later after many years, after the 19-year-old experience.

MICHAEL: I can imagine as you go booking performances and that kind of thing, that most concert halls would be expecting you to play this and this and this and this. This is going to happen at such-and-such a time. How do you deal with that, because what you're talking about and the way you're approaching your craft and your art is something that's totally outside of that usual linear planning process of a concert performance.

Which is why my answer to how I deal with that is that I have to be insane. I mean, it is insanity. What I have to do is kind of drag myself, and at a certain moment force it to produce something. I mean, there's no way to explain what I do. I've tried to do that, even explain it to myself. Luckily, it's something that can be done. It's as amazing to me as it is to people who wonder about it.

MICHAEL: Interesting word, insanity.

People have asked me what they have to do to do this, meaning hopefully, what they have to do to do something with as much commitment. I have to tell them that you first have to be insane. But being insane at the appropriate moment is really insane. It's super sane. I mean, it's too much, as they say.

PHIL: Keith, going back to a bit of our earlier conversation, many of us regard music like any art form, as a kind of conveyance, a communication of one type or another from the artist to whoever it is that's receiving the art. Especially if you think of things like pop songs or whatever, oftentimes it is an emotional communication, an expression of an emotion. Yet what you're talking about is something that transcends that and really is an experience in which all are present or party to it in a sense.

It's interesting when something conveys an emotion, like a song or a pop piece. While it's doing that, if it's clearly doing that, it's usually also becoming very quickly an object—a solid object that you can carry around with you. In the way things are right now, I think it's very important for people to realize that those objects are more illusory than the process that creates the objects. The process that creates the object is more than the emotion that the song is delivering. Even in the case of someone who writes object songs. I mean, I write, also. I compose, and the pieces become objects. But if I play a piece of another composer, I'm trying to deliver that piece from its solid nature back to being in the process of being written or played, or to make it vital again.

We all know how things tend to fall to the ground. Well, what I'm talking about is the fact that I think people are forgetting when I talk about point of entry—in a way it's misleading. There is no time that you are really entering anything. It's my fault for bringing it up, but I could clear that up. Entering the music is assuming the music is something to enter, but really the case is that the entering itself is the music. The rest are objects such as notes or dynamic markings or an attempt to convey an emotion. I think that everyone can convey emotions, because emotions are objects. Like colors are in a way something trustworthy and noticeable, but when you say what is the quality of clarity? I mean, what is the quality of colorlessness? It's hard to put that into words. So when I'm playing, or I think I could use a better term than "entering" it, would be to bring the music out of where it has come to where it continues to exist as a potential. So entering it was an easy way to do that one interview, but it isn't the right thing to use all the time.

MICHAEL: *It's like diving into the pool. As I listen to you talk about that, it occurs to me that there's a difference between a Van Cliburn playing Tchaikovsky's* Fifth Symphony *and the craft of that. That discipline and the kind of music you do improvisationally where what you have to do essentially is really jump off a cliff and trust. That where you are and what you're doing is going to occur the way it needs to occur. If one looks at other places around society, that's not the usual thing we see—jumping into the deep end of the pool. When you put yourself in front of 5,000 people who have paid good money to come into the auditorium, you're going to sit down and you're going to play right there. In the moment, it's going to happen. That's jumping into the deep end of the pool, for my money.*

Believe it or not, it's the same with interpreting other music, which is something I'm doing a lot more now and will be doing a lot more of in the future. The jumping in is exactly the same. In fact, there's no way to say which one of these things is more difficult. In order to play someone else's piece, you must first discipline yourself to this very precise ability to play a piece of music that someone else has written. If they're alive, they may be there to hear it, and if they're dead, you have respect for them because they will not write another piece. So you feel responsible. You first discipline yourself like a maniac. Then when it's time to play the piece, you have to say this is where I come from in terms of interpreting.

At that moment, when the piece is being played, I jump anyway. I am trusting in the discipline that I have already been going through, say the last few months working on this piece to take care of itself. You know, you can imagine from that description that is also an absolutely unbelievable thing when the piece wakes up. If the piece comes to life after you've jumped, you realize that it's so much more important to jump than to play this piece correctly. But yet you have to have used this correct discipline in order to at least be responsible to what has been written on this piece of paper. So there's another whole universe of incredibleness there.

I must say, though, that you cannot constantly be jumping. You know, you do land occasionally. Those times are when it's possible to get something accomplished that needs to be accomplished, or perhaps at the time of the next jump. If every jump were the same, then it wouldn't be a jump anymore; it would be security, as everything else would. Also, it's true that no one that I know is doing this, but I don't find that necessary. I'm a little bit appalled, in a way, that no one else is doing this. To me, the responsibility remains with the artists who are affecting these thousands of people. You know something that is not normal to them. Something that may be able to affect them more than having had a great time and whistling a melody as they leave.

MICHAEL: *Do you find new parts of yourself when you jump?*

I think every time. I think even if I don't want to, it has to be true. There's an example of what you could call "the law." If you jump, you discover something. If you jump with some landing place in mind, it doesn't count. It has to just be a jump.

PHIL: *Keith, I'm wondering if it might be interesting to talk a little bit more about some of those laws you described. I'm intrigued by that as an amateur musician myself, what that involves.*

Well, it doesn't involve anything I can describe in words. I mean, all I can say is that if we talk about jumping again, if you make the jump in a certain activity and other people are watching or listening or somehow participating in your jump, the quality of the jump will determine whether these laws hold true for these people. The stronger your intent and consciousness is at the moment of jumping, the more these people will have the same experience of this being whatever word they might use—*fantastic,* or I don't know what to say, or even if they say precise things like this happened to me. You will hear all of the people more or less saying the same thing.

The less potent you were at the time of the jump, the less that will be true. So the people that come to be entertained will perhaps say they were entertained; it was wonderful. The people that were potentially incredible listeners or participants will leave wondering the same things they wondered when they came. That's what I would call the typical artistic presentation. The limit at which Western society puts art is about there. Did you like it? You know, it would be my purpose to have someone leave saying, "What was that?" Not did you like it, not what was that, like "Gee, it's over my head," but "Leave me alone for a while." Two days, maybe.

MICHAEL: It might be useful to get into the process of jumping and what that jumping process involves. You have to give up who you think Keith Jarrett is when you make that jump, don't you?

Yes. That's a good topic that I'll try to briefly talk about. Not only do I have to give that up, but I have to accept it, also. So although I know an awful lot about music and can be my worst, most severe critic on the level that critics usually arrive at when they write their interviews, which I won't comment on at the moment, I cannot even be critical in the way they are about my performance or my music. If I'm going to let go and jump, I also have to let go of that. To let go of that means very often that I sound like myself. Even though I sound like myself to me for the very first time at that same time, I sound like myself for the 300th time to those critics whom I could be associating with, and I could well understand their condition at that moment. But they're not listening to the process or observing the process, usually. They're listening to the music and associating it. They don't know about jumping.

MICHAEL: *In other words, the jumping process is also an extremely personal and intimate process. You're making an agreement to share with others, but it's really a personal, intimate process.*

It's delicate, also. That leads to the legends surrounding my performances, where I stop and say something about, let's say, a cough or something. People are always thinking this is a personal thing. He's irritated. This is his nature. This has nothing to do with my nature; it has to do with the fact that I already jumped; and where I am is a delicate place. A delicate place is very easily tampered with beyond my control, and one of the things that can do that is a click of a camera. At that moment, I may have to stop because I just fell, you know. Really, that's a terrible situation.

MICHAEL: *Woke back up or went unconscious—one of the two.*

Yes, whatever it is. Even if that's not true, I owe it to the music to stop even if I'm still there. Sometimes it's just too much, you know. You have to say, well, they must know that part of the process demands something from them. But I'm not the only artist who sees cough contagion growing and growing. It's just that I might be more vocal.

MICHAEL: *We create wonderful ways to resist moving.*

Yes. We just recorded a concert in Amsterdam, which if it comes out, might have to have an apology on it for being probably the first great digital recording of a coughing audience. It's astounding. Every spare space is filled with a cough. Since the miking was so wonderful, we've got terrific coughs. Just terrific. If I had to prove this in court, all I would have to do is take this tape along.

MICHAEL: What do you think is going on?

Media is going on. Media is affecting people, with things that come into your homes and occupy all your senses at the same time. Then there's a commercial, and you have your coughing fit. You cough during anything, because the people on the movie screen or the television screen don't hear you. I think people resent the sensitivity of my position. It's a strange thing to say, but I think very often that's true.

MICHAEL: It's difficult to be in a sensitive position for an extended period of time. It takes discipline, and then intention and a commitment.

But they resent the fact that it's being done in front of them on their own time, in a way. That suddenly they're thrown into a situation where something is expected of them. They're almost defiant. There have been audiences that I could only say were defiant. They resisted at any cost the experience that they could've had. Because they thought I was feeling above them by coming and doing this for them, that they were sure I was going to tell them not to cough. So who is he to tell us not to cough? So you can see how the live situation can be, how it can get in the way of the jumps.

MICHAEL: We're dealing with small self, big self, ego, non-ego.

But amazingly, it works. We didn't learn it in school. It wasn't like I was surrounded with musicians who were saying yes, that's it. That was a jump. That wasn't a jump. People ask me what I listen to. I say I listen to music that, if I would rank it, I can only listen for any length of time to, let's say, number-one music. Otherwise, I'm wasting my time because I could be learning about the jump again. You know, my jump. But if I hear someone else who I can tell understands these processes, then it strengthens me. Everyone needs reminders from other places.

MICHAEL: *What happens when you make the jump and it really works, in the sense that you really get into it? Afterwards, what happens?*

Well, now I can deal with that. Some people are surprised that I'm back to normal life, and I'm not really, but I know how to. I mean it is an insanity. So mixing that insanity with the insanity we already have would make a little bit too potent a brew for continuing to do these things. So I guess I just have a few valves that operate at the right time. I didn't always. I also used to think one concert was good, another concert bad. Then I would find out that the one I thought was bad was wonderful, and the one I thought was good was pretty bad. I started to realize at that point that it was it was almost two selves who were arguing with each other. The one self had the experience on-stage. The other self is being critical of the music produced by the self on-stage. I choose the side of the self who said that it was good on-stage and bad on-stage. I don't choose the side of the person who listened to it afterwards and wants to deny one or the other. I think it's much more important while it's going on to have some sort of connection there. But most people don't. That's the reverse of what's usually considered normal.

MICHAEL: Sometimes we don't want to honor that part of our-selves. So we repress it and don't admit that it's there.

Why should the music be so good? Why should it just natu-rally follow that the music is wonderful if I've really gotten involved? I don't think that's necessarily going to follow. The music isn't always going to be wonderful music. It may be as vital an experience for me as I've ever had, but it may not make wonderful listening music on a record, which is one reason why solo concerts are becoming impossible to record.

MICHAEL: Why is it that solo concerts are becoming impossi-ble to record?

Because they are so much more the moment all the time, and so much less the music itself, that on records they don't have the kind of musicality.

MICHAEL: It reminds me of an experience I had in the San Francisco Opera House with Ravi Shankar doing a concert. It was the first time I had ever experienced what I would term an out-of-the-body mystical experience with music. I couldn't recre-ate that with the record of that experience. It was that experience then and there. That moment, the living moment when that was happening.

That's right. But you see, I'm sure so many people miss this point. The experience you had you cannot erase. The important thing is whether someone had an experience that they can use. Otherwise, what's the purpose of art? I don't see any purpose in art. I mean, if society is the way it is now with all the master-pieces that already exist, then masterpieces aren't what it's about.

MICHAEL: *Right. Well, that particular experience blew my mind and produced some distinct changes in my life.*

PHIL: *With respect to that last point about your relationship with your audience, and also in connection with what you were saying earlier, what's really the purpose of doing what you do in public, both in records and concerts? I gather that it is to try and make that kind of experience possible.*

Right. But interestingly enough, I'm stopping solo concerts very, very shortly for an undetermined period of time because since what we just said about the mind is true, it can always find a way to outsmart our own experience. Whole audiences are finding a way to do that with solo concerts, and so the only solution for me is to take them off the market. It isn't a negative thing, but you can imagine why that might be necessary. The expectation is that instead of there being no expectations, now there are new expectations. For me, I just don't want to play that game. I'd rather just make music. So I'm now making other people's music more than my own. The jump is the same.

PHIL: *I was wondering earlier when you were talking about how the media affects our sensibility how long you could continue to wage, in a sense, a battle against that.*

Not forever. Not in one area forever, because people will just refurbish their new homes and live in them and bring them along. So I do not think that playing so often is really healthy for me in terms of what I need. I'm now asking myself what I need, since this is becoming an item again. Maybe if it's not there for a while, people will have their own internal combustion chambers. Actually, the ideal thing would have been to play one solo concert in each city and stop. Not say a word. People need space.

They need time and space to have their own relationships to things. Now it's like, when is the next one? Well, I don't know. Not next year. Oh, gee, maybe he's trying to tell us something.

MICHAEL: Do you find the writing process very similar to the jumping-off or solo concert process? I mean, it takes a jump, too, doesn't it?

The first mark on the score paper, yes. It's a gigantic jump, and I usually am jumping all over the place through a written piece. But it isn't quite the same. If a piece is really important, it demands looking at it over a long period of time. That's not true of a solo concert necessarily. I think for a piece to be good, it has so many jumps in it that you need to hear this piece many times and hear it played by different people. As a composer, that's the gift you get. Can other people see what's here? Assuming the composer likes what he's written. Most composers never get to hear their pieces played by people who see what's there.

I've felt very good about playing a few living composers' pieces who knew that I knew where their jumps were or what kind of experience they were trying to show through their music. That's been a real pleasure for me. I wish some other people who are not alive were still alive. We don't all have the kind of training to play solo concerts. It's just lucky that I can be as healthy as I am. Otherwise I couldn't jump in quite the whole way that I do.

MICHAEL: Earlier you mentioned that you were surprised that there weren't other artists doing what you're doing. We were talking about that a little bit to some extent in other fields and other professions. We don't see much of that kind of willingness to be spontaneous and to dive in. Have other artists asked you about what you do and say, Well, how do you that, man? Then can I do that?

No. Not at all.

MICHAEL: *It's amazing.*

I'll tell you what the main attitude is. It's that it's a freak thing. Other musicians write it off; they want to write it off very badly. First of all, most people are envious of the success story. That coupled with the fact that they want to write it off somehow. So oftentimes they'll be just saying, Oh, well, Keith, yeah. Well, he does that, you know, but nobody else does that.

It's just really unique. It's different.

MICHAEL: *I think my own sense would be that the commercial success might provide some momentum to say, Well, gee, maybe there is something there.*

That has happened, but on an even more silly level than what I was really relating. I mean, there are imitations of the notes now, of the kind of sequence of notes that might have been on an earlier solo concert by people who would never have had a chance to record without my wonderful example, which I feel very responsible for. It's another good reason to take these concerts out of the so-called public eye and let this stuff do what it's going to do. It is strange that people will if they want to, let's say, if they want to emulate someone or they look they have some respect for someone. They still want to fit that thing that guy does or that person does into their own limits. So-and-so has his own limits at this moment, and he would like to be doing such-and-such a thing, but he doesn't want to do it enough that it will change his own limits. The only thing I'm trying to do is change my limits. So if someone is going to imitate me, I would appreciate it if they at least look at it that way. Then we would have some other people doing it. Then I wouldn't have to talk as though I'm a freak, you know. I'd love to hear someone else do this.

MICHAEL: Oh, I don't think you're a freak, Keith. I think you're doing something that's very sane.

Well, I don't think so, either, but I'm using that term because I've actually heard it a few times. I don't know if I should mention a name, but a very famous musician who at one time was supposedly a jazz pianist and who now is conducting, which gives away the whole thing, was asked what he thought of my solo work. He said anybody that plays for 45 minutes is bound to come up with something. So you know, I consider that a write-off because he hasn't tried it. Or maybe in the privacy of his home. But the sad thing is that waking up is so difficult, you know. If I meet someone who's awake, I hope I know it. I hope I don't close the door. I mean, I hope that there's something that I could gain rather than feeling let's keep this separate from me. Let's keep this over here in this corner. I'll be me and he'll be him, and everything will be fine. I'll read a wonderful book and gain what I am capable of gaining. I don't want to gain any more from it because it might be uncomfortable. It's too bad.

MICHAEL: I've got to watch out. I might discover something about myself.

Yeah. The knock on the door isn't going to happen. I'm sure if I had ignored the experience at 19, it's very conceivable that I would never have had those converging lines at another time. There's no doubt that even if I were in music I wouldn't know what I was doing. I mean, I probably would not know what I was doing.

MICHAEL: *We all need to become more conscious of the present moment. More aware of what's going on now.*

And the potential of the moment. Not so much what's happening in the moment. What's happening in the moment is the potential in a way that the atom bomb is the reverse side of the potential of the moment. The atom bomb is the kinetic force of the moment of the second. It's the process of creativity, but backwards in a way. Creativity, I think, is the awareness of the potential of the moment. If you have a tool to present that to someone, you present it in a very, very watered-down version from what you really feel. I can't make the music be what I feel. It's a watered-down, diluted version, but if I can keep the potential of the moment alive in the music, then that music is valuable to a listener. If I can't, it's not. If I can't, it becomes an object as an atom bomb is an object. It is potentially destructive, because someone who listens to it will hear it, and it will not be alive. What they're listening to will not be alive. They will think, Well, it's better than this other thing I heard, which was even more dead. But it will still not be alive. They will not hear creativity as it's meant to be.

🔱   🔱   🔱

EPILOGUE

"The only thing I'm trying to do is change my limits," and thus Keith Jarrett reveals the purpose of living at the creative edge, realizing the potential of each moment. This requires a willingness to trust, to be spontaneous in the moment and allow whatever wants to happen, simply to emerge. You don't have to make anything happen, just let go and be. The creative possibilities are limitless, and if we're able to fully enter the unmapped territory of the moment, then anything can happen. Self-imposed limits disappear, and new creative vistas are possible. As an accomplished musical artist whose spontaneous, unrehearsed concerts are legendary, Keith Jarrett shows the way to plumb the depths of our creativity, no matter what our chosen path may be.

CHAPTER FIVE

❦　　❦　　❦

The Art of Storytelling

Isabel Allende, with Michael Toms

PROLOGUE

*T*he *storyteller has been a fixture in human affairs far longer than anyone remembers. Surely even in prehistoric times we can imagine the hunter tale being shared around the warmth of a fire. For millennia we have learned from stories. Good stories could carry the listener or reader into imaginary realities or real-life adventures. The ability to affect the heart and mind is powerful magic.*

A little more than a decade ago, in 1985, the stories of Isabel Allende burst upon the world with a seldom-seen fire and passion. The House of Spirits *chronicled four generations of a Chilean family against the backdrop of Chile's brutal history. Then, Isabel's first work of nonfiction appeared,* Paula, *a soul-bearing autobiographical account of the wrenching experience of her daughter dying. It is a compelling story. Following her impressive debut with* The House of Spirits, *other books came.* Of Love and Shadows, Eva Luna, The Stories of Eva Luna, *and* The Infinite Plan—all bestsellers around the world.

Isabel Allende was born in Lima, Peru, and raised in Chile, Bolivia, Europe, and the Middle East, as her family followed her stepfather's diplomatic career. She worked as a journalist in Chile until the 1973 military coup, when she left her homeland.

🔱　🔱　🔱

MICHAEL TOMS: *Isabel, you began writing as a journalist, and then you left Chile and you didn't write for a long time. How did you suddenly become a fiction writer?*

ISABEL ALLENDE: I think I didn't have a choice. I had all these events stuck in my chest, all these unwritten events and unwritten words. I had been in silence for a very long time, paralyzed by the experience of exile and the losses in my life. Then one day it was January 8, 1981, and I heard that my grandfather was dying in Chile. He was the most important male figure in my life—when I was little, at least. I began a letter. It was sort of a spiritual letter to say good-bye and tell him that he could go in peace because I had all the anecdotes that he had told me, all his memories with me. I had not forgotten anything. To prove that, to prove that life goes on and memory is important, I started writing the first anecdote he ever told me. That was the story of my aunt Rose, who everybody said was very beautiful. Then something happened, and the letter became something else. I started stealing other people's lives, and other characters stepped in, and it was fiction all of a sudden, but I didn't know what it was. To me it was still a letter. When I had 500 pages on the dining room table, I realized that it didn't look like a letter anymore, and my grandfather had died, so he was never going to receive it.

When you suddenly realized that you had a book on your hands, was it easy to get it published?

No it was very difficult. I didn't know it was a book. I gave it to my mother. My mother said, "I don't know, but this looks like a novel to me." She helped me correct the grammar and other stuff. Then I submitted it to several publishers in Latin America. No one wanted to read it. This was the first novel, very long, a very dirty manuscript; no one knew me, and I had a very political name. So it was a risky thing for any publisher. Then the secretary in a publishing house called me one day and said, "We are never going to publish this book, but they're not going to tell you this. I think this book is good, why don't you send it to an agent." I didn't know that agents existed for books. I thought they were only for sports. So I sent the book to someone she recommended in Barcelona. She had the book published, translated, reviewed, distributed. So I was very lucky that it was not published in Latin America.

When you start out a book, how do you start writing?

I have a ceremony on January 8th—I always start my books the same day. I have a sort of a ceremony that has become more and more complicated every time. You know, writing a novel is a long pursuit. It can last two or three years. You really have to be in love with it, and you really have to befriend the spirits of the book. The characters have to walk into your life, into the space where you're going to write, and I have to welcome them. I need help. I need inspiration, so I have my mother, my daughter, who died recently, and my grandmother to help me. I welcome them. I ask for help.

Every morning when I write, I light a candle for them; they are there, their photographs are there with me. I get in the mood of writing by writing a letter to my mother every morning. Then I just open my heart, if you can call it that. It sounds tacky, but that's the way it is. When I start a book, I write a first sentence. Usually I don't know what a first sentence is. Sometimes I think that I have a first sentence for a novel that I'm planning, then I write that sentence and it's another thing. It's totally different, and I realize that I will write something else. So I let myself go. I'm very open to that experience, and I pour out the story in a first draft that is very messy and very long. I don't know what the story's about until I print it and I read it. Then I say, Ah, this is what it is, and then I start cleaning up, eliminating, correcting. Then I write a second draft. The third draft is for language. When I think it's more or less okay, I send it to my mother in Chile. She reads it, takes the first plane, comes here with a red pen, and we fight for a month, at least. We fight and then she leaves, and of the 600 pages I had originally, I have like 15 left. Then I start working again.

Was your mother always an editor?

No. My mother is tough. She's a tough critic, and she loves me unconditionally. So she will be very honest with me. She doesn't have to be careful. She can say anything she wants, and I know that it's always with the best of intentions. So although I don't pay attention to everything she says, I know that if she doesn't like something, there is something wrong. She can say for example, I don't like the ending. But she can't say what would be a better ending. But if she doesn't like the ending, it's because it's not working. So I write it over and over again until I feel that I've found what is the best, or better at least. She also has an eye for clichés and a sense of irony. She always sees things from behind, and that's great, so that I won't fall into the stereotype. She will tell me immediately, no, this is just a cliché of the character, and she will force me to go deeper and deeper into the soul.

Would you say your books have a message behind them?

No. I don't intend to deliver any sort of message, because I don't have any answers. I just have the questions, and these are the same questions that everybody's asking. Maybe what a writer has to do at a certain time is just tune into the question and repeat it in such a way that it will have a ripple effect and touch more people. But I don't have messages. I don't know the answers, and I'm always moved by the same themes, the same things. So by going over and over again through the same questions, I'm asking myself who I am. It's sort of, I don't know how to call it, but it's like a journey inside yourself. I suppose you do that in therapy, also. I do it through my writing.

You've described yourself as an insatiable story hunter. What do you mean by that?

I'm stealing other people's lives. Beware, whatever you say can be used against you. I meet someone, and I want to know what happened and why in their lives. I ask always the wrong questions, but I am lucky and I ask them to the right people. So I get stories. Through other people's stories, I intend to make clear things for myself.

So the people who appear in your books are real people?

I always write fiction and I can't trace the boundary between reality and fantasy anymore. The stories are always based on some form of real people or real life, but I turn them around and twist them and deform them, and it's always fiction. So I don't know. I don't know how to answer that. I suppose they're not real people.

But you do this with your friends as well; you take their stories, right?

Yes. I take my friends' stories, but I'm careful. I'm careful not to betray them, and for me a friend is more important than a character. A person is always more important than a character, so I try not to betray them. I never use another person's story unless I've been authorized to do it.

What do you think the importance is of telling stories?

I think that stories are to the big audience, to the readers, to the society, what dreams are to individuals. They clear up the fog in our minds. If you don't dream, you go mad. Dreams somehow unclog your mind and help you tune into the unconscious world from where you can draw experience and information. I think that's what stories do. There are hundreds, thousands, but we are always repeating the same stories. All the great plots have already been told innumerable times. We can only tell them again in a different way, but every time we do that, we tune into the myth. Somehow we make the society dream, and maybe that's why stories are important. I mean, just once say, "Once upon a time" in an elevator, and no one will get off the elevator. You remain there until you finish the story. The power of storytelling is amazing.

It probably goes back to childhood, because we all had someone tell us a story.

What did the people of the Stone Age do? Sit around the fire in those long winters and tell stories.

Yes, it's certainly been with us since human beings have been around, I'm sure. The oral tradition, a very powerful tradition.

Speaking of traditions, you're from South America, and there's a very different family life that goes on in there. You're a fairly recent arrival in the United States. How do you see the difference between family life in South America and family life in the United States?

On family life, there are two aspects: one that is very attractive to me, and one that I reject completely. In Latin America, we all belong in an extended family, or a tribe, a clan, or a village. Somehow there is a network of support. You are never all by yourself, because whatever happens, it's not the state or the insurance company that will take care of you; it's the family, this network of relationships. So you are supported and helped, but at the same time, you have a burden of responsibility toward that group. There's no way that you can ever get away from that. It's a sense of honor. For example, I'm called Allende. I carry Salvador Allende's family name, and so I have a sense of honor and of shame that I will never do something that will harm that name, because I'm not alone. I represent something.

If I get rich, everybody gets rich with me, because I carry everybody with me. If I'm poor, the rest of the people will have to support me and help me. So that's the good part of it. The bad part is that you're never free. In this country, you cross the border of the state, you change your name, you change your clothes, and you become another person. You see that in the movies, on television all the time. It's like the American dream. You go farther west and you begin again, and there are no memories, no guilt, no shame, no family, no bonds; you're alone. So the myth of the lonely ranger is still alive. It's still present in our lives. That gives you a sense of freedom and power, but also of terrible loneliness. So it's these two aspects—the positive aspect is that you have the support and you are related, and whatever you do affects the group. You belong somewhere. The bad part is that you're never free.

It strikes me that your work emerges from deep feeling, and in some cases, pain and anguish. Do you see your work coming out of your own pain, your own anguish?

I think that every book is triggered by a very strong emotion that has been with me for a very long time. Usually that emotion is painful. However, the process of writing is so joyful. It's like an orgy that I can't explain. I have a great time writing. I can write 14 hours a day and not eat anything for 14 hours, and yet I feel wonderful because the process is so wonderful. What triggers it and the emotion is painful. I often cry when I write.

Do you think that's true for most writers, that there's this kind of myth almost about how one has to suffer in order to be creative? Do you think that's true?

No. I think that you are more creative when you have free time, when you have solved your basic needs. When you are not at the level of survival. When you have affection and support and when you are free. I think that's the best creative mood.

You are a great believer in solitude for writing. Please tell us about that.

Well, writing requires concentration and silence. I can only get that in total solitude. If I don't have the sort of womb where I work and I can't retreat completely, then I can't write. I can write journalism, letters, speeches, but I can't write fiction. Because fiction is like embroidering a tapestry. You go little by little with a very fine needle, with threads of different colors. You need concentration because you don't have the pattern; you don't know the pattern. You can't leave any threads loose. You have to tie them all. You can't see the knots. So that requires you to have everything in your mind. Maybe other writers have an outline and they follow the outline, and that way they don't really need that kind of concentration, but I'm incapable of doing that. Writing happens one line at time, so I have to keep in mind the previous line and the line that I wrote first three months ago so that the whole story will be clean at the end.

I recall a story you told about one of the accounts, I think it was in The House of the Spirits, *about the mind. You wrote about how the peasants had been murdered and later encountered a priest. It reminds me that through your work, and when I hear you talk about your inspiration, there's a psychic thread that moves through your process. Can you tell us that story, first of all, and maybe our readers will better understand?*

That story is from *Of Love and Shadow,* and what triggered that book was anger—anger at the abuses of the dictatorship in Chile. They had killed many people, and many people had disappeared, and their bodies were never found. This is a story of a political crime that happened in 1973 in Chile. Fifteen persons were murdered, and their bodies were hidden. Five years later, the Catholic church opened an abandoned mine and found the bodies. No one knows how they got the news, and how they could open it before the police could stop them. But that's how I learned about it, because it was in the news and there was a trial.

When I wrote the story, I only had the information that the Chilean government had released, which was very partial. I had to fill up the gaps with imagination. When I finished the story, my mother read the book and she said, "Look, this is totally, totally unbelievable. The fact that a priest learns in confession that the bodies are in the mine, his brother takes his motorcycle, goes there during curfew to a place that has been closed by the police, opens the mine, finds the bodies, photographs them and brings the photographs to the Cardinal, that's totally unbelievable." I said, "Mom, it's a literary device. I have no other way of solving the plot." The book was published in 1984. I could return to Chile in 1988. When I did that, a Jesuit priest came to speak with me and he said he had learned in confession that the bodies were in the mine. He had gone there during curfew on his motorcycle, opened the mine, photographed the bodies, and taken the photographs to the Cardinal. That's how the Catholic church opened the mine before they were stopped by the authorities. He asked me how I had known, because the only people who knew about this were the Cardinal and himself. I don't know how I knew. I thought I had made it up.

It's like you're tapping into another level of consciousness or another reality. When you write, somehow it creates a linear sequence to events, and that's not the same as what's in our minds, which in some ways is timeless. No past. No present. No future. It's all timeless inside. Is that the way it works for you?

Yes. It's like a book that contains all the story, but you open the page, any page, and you see just fragments of the story. But in your memory or in your soul, all the book is already written, all the stories already lived. When I write, sometimes I feel that I tap into something that will happen in the future. I say in one part of this book that I'm remembering what has not happened and what will happen. Because in a way that's how I feel when I write a story, even if it's my own story. That my story already happened, and I know it at an instinctual level. It's just that I haven't opened the right page yet, but it's there. It's written already.

The book Paula *actually began with a letter to your daughter, didn't it?*

Yes. In December 1991, I was visiting Madrid for the pre-sentation of my book *The Infinite Plan,* my last novel. I was at a party in Barcelona where the publishing house was presenting the book to the press, and someone came over and whispered in my ear that Paula was in the hospital. So I rushed to the hospital and forgot about the book, forgot about my life, forgot about every-thing. For the next year, I was at my daughter's bedside. She fell into a coma. She had a condition called porphyry. It's a very rare condition. Very few people know what it is. You can live all your life with that. She took very good care of herself. She knew she had it, but unfortunately several things coincided: She had the flu, she was stressed out, she was vomiting, she had hormonal changes at the time—all that triggered a porphyria attack.

When she went to the hospital, she said she had porphyria, and no one had heard of it. So they gave her the wrong drugs, and she fell into a coma and never woke up. The doctors kept on say-ing that she would snap out of it suddenly and that was what sometimes happened with these porphyric patients. It took five-and-a-half months for them to admit that she had severe brain damage and would never wake up. At that point, I disconnected her from the respirator, and she started breathing, so I brought her home in an incredible trip by plane from Madrid to San Rafael where I lived. There we took care of her until she died.

In the meantime, I was writing a letter for her. The letter began in the hospital, in Madrid, because I was convinced that she was going to wake up and I thought that maybe she would have lapses in her memory and she would not remember what had happened. The intention of the letter in the beginning was to bring to her all the memories of her life and my life and her coun-try and her family and her husband and everything that had hap-pened in our lives. So two stories intertwined in these pages—her story in the hospital, her agony and death, and the story of my life and my extended family. So it's a strange book, braided in a strange way.

Previously, all of your books had been fiction, and this book is an autobiographical account of your life, as well as Paula's life. I'm wondering how that was for you—knowing that you're switching from fiction to nonfiction?

I wasn't writing a book. I was writing a sort of journal for Paula. I never had the intention to publish it. When Paula died, exactly a year after she fell into a coma, and that is December 6, 1992, I think that I was in a strange state of mind. Probably heartbroken and in shock, and because this had been so long, I think that I was hallucinating. I was seeing things and feelings things and dreaming. It was a state of hypersensibility. My mother came, of course, immediately. A month later, January 8, 1993—that's the date when I usually start my books—my mother said, "You have to start another book." I said, "Mom, I will never be able to write again." She said, "Yes, you will, but you have to try. The only way that you can go through this pain is imagining that this is a tunnel and be absolutely convinced because I'm telling you so that there is light at the other end. But you can't see it right now, just keep on walking. Then at one point you will start feeling that there is first a breeze of fresh air, and then finally you will see the light and you will come out of this. Your way of mourning is writing, because this is the only thing that you can do and you know how to do."

So I started to write. I had planned a novel, of course, because I'm a fiction writer, and I feel very happy when I'm telling stories. However, I could not. When I turned on the computer on January 8th, the first sentence that came was written by itself. I didn't write it. It just appeared on the screen, and it was: *Listen Paula, I'm going to tell you a story so that when you wake up you will not be so lost.* That was the first sentence I had written in the hospital when she fell sick a year before. So I said, Well, I'm going to rewrite this letter and add all the letters that I wrote to my mother. The letters that Ernesto and Paula shared as lovers and all the information I have. I produced something that I didn't know very well. I knew it was not fiction. Then with my mother and with the rest of the family, we decided that this was an important book to publish. Although my mother, of course, said that this is very revealing, and you don't want to tell the world that you have had lovers or anything of the sort, I really tried to edit it and take away some things, and I couldn't. I felt that each time I tried, I was betraying the spirit of the book. So I thought, No, either it's published the way it is, or it's not published. Fortunately, other people mentioned in the book accepted having their names and their stories in it.

You mentioned your mother many times in this written account. Can you tell us about your relationship with your mother. She's been a very powerful influence.

My mother, my daughter and I, we come from a lineage of very strong women. In my family, more males than females are born. So the women have to be very organized, very loving, and very close so that they can cope with all these macho patriarchal authoritarians that I belong to. My grandmother started this tradition, my mother followed it, and I have been like one part of that chain. The way we did it when Paula was alive, is that I would write a letter every day for my mother and Paula and send a copy to each. They'd read the same thing. Paula did not write every day, she would write like twice a week. But my mother because she has more time, can write even two letters a day. That way we have kept in touch for 35 years, my mother and I, this incredible correspondence. We also talk on the phone, fax each other now, and we see each other a lot. She's the person who edits my books and corrects them. She's the only person who confronts me with the writing before the book's published. So she's a very important person in my life. She's tough.

Going back to the writing, in the writing of the letter to Paula, did you find that that was a way to deal with your grief and grieving? I mean, it had to be intense as you were there with her.

While she was sick, to write was sort of a relief. I was so obsessed with her, so stressed out, that those hours that I was writing were the hours that were mine. I was distracted, and I was happy writing, remembering. Somehow I found a lot of strength in the memories of all those people that had been in my life and all those stories and all those adventures. I have had a wonderful life, full of fun and stress and success and great failures and great losses and great love. So all that came together in those pages, and I could see the pattern of my life. I could see that it was a life well lived in a way, and that made me very happy. Later, after Paula died and I rewrote all this, it was my way of mourning, of being with Paula, but it was also a happy time. I would cry a lot, but I would laugh. I was also distracted for many hours a day.

So really, Michael, the only thing that I can do is tell stories. Even if I'm telling my own story, it's a way of recreating reality. There is an artifice, there are lies also in this book that is nonfiction, and I believe that everything in the book is true. But there is one basic lie, the fact that you're writing it down. That is something artificial, because life doesn't happen that way. Memories are not that way. Everything happens simultaneously. You see everything from every angle. You see everything in different ways, and if you try to establish a chronological order or whatever order you choose in the writing, it's all artificial. That helps me in a way, because it makes me understand how circles close, even if it's in an artificial way. Who I am, where I stand. It sorts out a little bit of the confusion. On the other hand, when I rewrote the book, I knew the ending. When I started writing it, I didn't. I wanted a happy ending. When I rewrote it, I knew that there was no happy ending because Paula had died. However, when I finished writing it, I realized that it was a happy ending. This is a book with a happy ending with Paula liberated. With Paula alive in a different way, in a different dimension and with me.

In some way, now that the book is out, she lives on. Her story and the power of her life lives on.

Yes. She comes back to me in weird ways. First of all, the book in Spanish, Italian, Dutch, and many other languages has been published with her photograph on the jacket, so she's there on tables and chairs and beds and people's hands on the buses. She's alive in a way. She's sharing her life with many people. I'm getting an incredible amount of letters from South America and Europe, and in many of the letters, there's sometimes a sentence that is like her talking to me from another world, from another time. She comes back and says to me in an ironic way the kind of things that she used to say. For example, one thing that many letters repeat over and over is: "Keep on writing. On January 8th, I will be praying for you so that you will be writing." We have this joke with my daughter. She would call me from anywhere in the world where she would be. She would call me on January 7th and say, "Vieja, start writing." She would always have some ironic thing to say about that. So on January 7th, I got faxes, letters, phone calls—I can't imagine the mail that day. People saying keep on writing. So it was her reminding me to keep on writing.

How was that process for you? You know, being with your daughter in the course of a year while she was in a coma?

Stages, just different stages. At the beginning, hope. Struggling like a samurai to bring her back to life. Then slowly giving up. First giving up her body and saying, Well, she's not going to be the beautiful, graceful, wonderful girl she was. Then

I said that it doesn't matter, we still have the rest. Then giving up the mind. When I learned that she had severe brain damage and she would never recover, I said okay, the mind is not so important, I'll take care of her. We still have her alive, and she's still here. Then also giving up that and saying, Okay, she can go and I will not love her less for that. I told her that she could go, that I loved her very much, and I was going to be with her here and somewhere else in the future. So then I have some ashes, and then I didn't even have that.

Isabel, do you have something else you'd like to say about your daughter?

I get very emotional when I talk about this, but I know that many people have realities where people they love in a similar situation are dying or very sick. Maybe my experience will be useful to them. After a while, you lose the fear of death. Not only that your daughter will die, but that you yourself will die. You realize that death is like being born. It's like a threshold that you cross into another world, and you don't carry any memories with you. That's why it's so frightening. But there is nothing frightening in the fact that you die. Paula died in my arms. I got in bed with her and held her for a day and a night until she died.

When she died, I had this feeling of peace so profound that I fell asleep. I still remember the dream I had when I was holding her, and she was dead. My son woke me up: "We have to dress her and clean her," he said. We did that, and we decided not to take her out of the house until her husband came. Her husband was in Chicago. She stayed with us, the body stayed with us for two days, and I was with her. In those two days, I got acquainted with death. There's nothing frightening about it. It's painful for me now to know that there's no telephone number where I can reach my daughter, that I will never talk to her again. I will never hear her laughter, but she exists, the spirit exists and is connected to mine. I'm not scared of her death or mine. I'm not scared of the death of any of the people that I love.

That's one of the things I get from reading what you write— that you seem not to have a fear of death any longer.

Not anymore. Not anymore at all. But I'm sure that you feel the same way, Michael. I was more fortunate than you because I could be with Paula in the last moments of her life. I could accompany her to the threshold of death and be with her. In a way, I have the feeling that I had a glimpse of how it is on the other side. I lost the fear of death completely. My death and the people around me who feel that I can't control anything. I can't protect anybody. I can only love them in a very unconditional and wonderful way. I don't mind my own death at all. I know that it's not the opposite of life, it's the complement. It's not the opposite side of the coin; it's the same coin. If you are not afraid of death, what can you be afraid of? I'm afraid of unnecessary violence, but that's practically the only thing.

Someone said that there's birth and death, and both are in the process of life.

Yes. You know, I'm so fortunate that my granddaughter was born a few days before I brought Paula into that room—in the same room where Paula died six months later. I had in the same space this wonderful experience of birth and death, of two creatures who are very close to my heart, the closest to my heart. My daughter-in-law allowed me to be the midwife for her. I trained myself, and I was able to receive my granddaughter, cut the umbilical cord, and hold her—the first person who held her in the world. I remember that the first thing that came out of that incredibly sacred and wonderful moment was a question. The question was: *Tell me where you come from before you forget.*

I had this absolute certainty that she was coming from a place and that place was not her mother's womb. That place was something else, a spiritual ocean of consciousness, of awareness, of spirituality that she had been embodied and would come through this door that her mother was. I had exactly the same experience when Paula was leaving. That in a way I had been the door, the threshold, through which she came into the world. She had to do something here for 28 years, and then I was holding her when she was leaving to go to another place that was like the place she had come from. Like the place my granddaughter, Andrea, had come from a few months before. So there was no fear, just the desire to tell Paula that it was going to be okay because she knew the place. It was not going to be darkness and despair, but a wonderful place.

It leads me to ask you about your own spiritual practice. What would you say your spiritual view is?

I'm not a religious person. I don't belong to any organized, traditional religion. I wish I had faith. I think that faith is a gift. If you believe in any religion or in a certain God that is pre-established, things are clear. You don't have to make so many choices. You don't have to question everything. But I don't have that privilege, so I keep on inventing my own gods and goddesses. I have a spiritual practice that I have put together because I need it. I need to meditate. I need to pray to this thing that is spiritual in me. But I have to carry inside myself a moral structure that is so solid that guides me because I don't accept the rules of any religion. It's hard. Sometimes it is hard.

You don't think there's a difference between spirituality and religion?

Yes, both things are confused often. I come from a very Catholic background. So the fact that I question God is terrible, for example, for my mother, but I just don't feel comfortable with the gods that we have created, especially the male gods. The idea that God would have gender is just preposterous. It's like if God has genitals, he must have a digestive system, too, wouldn't he? And tonsils and a liver. I mean, it's just stupid.

Yes. When we realize that religion has come out of the experience that is really beyond words and the mystery. Religion is set up basically to preserve or to recreate rituals that remind us of that experience. The experience is beyond dogma and data.

Also, the experience is very personal. I think it's directly related to pain. That's why this idea that we should avoid pain no matter what is crazy, because it separates us from the experience of the sacred. We are in touch with the deepest part of ourselves through pain, very often, and extreme love. But love and pain are also related. Why am I in so much pain about Paula? Because I loved her so much. Both things are so related that I just can't separate them. This experience of pain and love has brought me to a spiritual dimension in my life that I probably didn't need before when everything seemed to be happy.

I recall reading an interview of yours somewhere when someone asked you the question about your philosophy of life. You talked about how when you're at the peak of your success, you also remember that pain may come in the future.

It usually comes immediately after the peak. I seem to go from one extreme to the other, up and down. My life is like that, and I accept that. I don't try to avoid the success and great moments and the love and the passion or the pain, the losses, the failures. It's also part of my life. I am the person I am because of those things.

In addition to your own experiences, are there any other Latin American writers who have influenced you in your work?

Many. All of them. I belong to the first generation of Latin American writers to be brought up reading other writers from our continent. The previous generation, the generation of the boom, grew up reading European and American writers in translation. But I was influenced by all of them: Gabriel Garcia Marquez, Carlos Fuentes, Mario Vargas Llosa, so many of them. Some of my own generation, such as Eduardo Galeeno, and many others whom I have read and have given me a paved way. It's easy for me to write because I don't have to invent anything; they already found a voice, a way of telling us to ourselves.

What about Pablo Neruda?

He's been an influence in my life, but perhaps not in my writing. Pablo Neruda is a poet of the senses. He talks about, for example, an ode to oil. You've been using oil all your life, but you've never seen it. You've never seen the transparency, the color, the texture, the smell. You don't know where it comes from or how it's made and all the beautiful textures; the fabric of oil becomes real to you when you really know that. In a way, I have tried to use that in my life. I don't take anything for granted.

Let me tell you the most sensuous thing that has ever happened to me. I'm 50, and I have had a lot of wonderful experiences, and one of my favorite is having a bath with my grandchildren. I'm sure Neruda would have written a long poem about that. Every time I eat something or I drink or I walk in nature, I remember Neruda and I say, Gosh, it's not only seeing, smell, taste, putting things in your mouth—listen. Be quiet and listen. Touch. Smell the flowers.

I think one of the gifts that Latin American writers can share with those of us who live in North America is the sense of the heart and soul that comes through their writing. There's a quality that reminds me of the rain forest, the richness and luxuriant quality of the rain forest.

But I think that you find that in many North American writers, especially women, minority groups. Black women, Chicano, Chinese-American, Japanese-American, Native American—you find that kind of writing all the time.

What other influences would you say your writing has?

The movies. An image in a movie, a color sometimes, can trigger a whole story. Nature is very important. I think that one is determined by the place where one is born. I was born among mountains. I'm a mountain person. I'm not a beach or tropical beach, not a palm tree person. I come from a very abrupt geography, from the Andes and the Pacific Ocean. That's why I feel so comfortable in California, because it looks similar in some areas. I come from a country of geographical and political catastrophes; nothing is ever secure for us. That feeling of uncertainty, of always finding your way in a labyrinth, has also determined my life and my writing.

At one point, you wrote or said something about the contract between the reader and the author. Can you talk a little bit about that?

Well, in Sudan, the storyteller sits in the center of the village and she says, I'm going to tell you a story, and the people say, Right. Not everything in the story is true. Right. But then not everything is false either. Right. They have a sort of contract, you see. She tells the story, and we know the rules. Not everything is believable, but we're going to pretend that it is. Well, that's how I feel with my readers. I'm proposing something. I'm saying, Hey, this is the story I'm going to tell. Not everything is true, not everything is false. But maybe in this bunch of lies we can find some particles of truth. Let's both enter into this dimension of literature that is similar to reality, but is not all together real and pretend it is and find our way together. That's what writing is. I mean, I can't imagine writing for myself or writing and not publishing. Because I feel that a book doesn't exist in itself. It's not an end in itself. It's just a way of communicating, a bridge. If I don't have a reader, and I don't find someone to hold my hand and explore together this space and time of the book, then I'm not interested, really. I would rather do something else.

As you're writing, do you think about the writer as you write?

I think about one reader. I don't think of large audiences or millions of copies. I don't care. But I want to touch one person's heart, take that person, grab that person, and say, "I'm not going to let you go until the end of the book. You will read until the last page." That's important to me, very important.

Have you been surprised by the success of your books?

Yes. Very surprised. I'm surprised by the fact that so many young people read me, people in different places. My books have been translated to more than 27 languages. It's amazing that we have so many similarities. The similarities are so many more than the differences, if you think about it.

So the story is universal. It goes around the world.

If you talk about emotions and passions and obsessions, it's always the same thing.

In The Infinite Plan, *you had a chapter in there about Berkeley in the sixties. Now you weren't here in Berkeley at that time, so how did you find out about Berkeley in the sixties?*

I had a friend who was in Berkeley in the sixties. She took me back to Berkeley, and we walked in the streets and talked to the street people. The same people have been there for 20 years. She told me her story and allowed me to write about it. Many other people in the street told me their stories, too. So that was easy. The chapter on Vietnam was more difficult. I wrote the chapter twice. I felt that I was ready to eliminate it from the book because all the information was there, too much information, and no real feeling because I can't relate to the experience of war. Being a woman and being the kind of person I am, so anti-militarism, it's very difficult. It's very difficult to relate to that, but I'm lucky. At the point when I was ready to take the chapter out, a Vietnam vet walked into my life, and he gave me the wonderful gift of this experience. I recorded it. My job was to translate it into Spanish.

So again, it's the happening of other people's stories.

I take many things. For example, I have even taken some parts of my husband's life. Now fiction sometimes is more powerful than reality. Who knows? In some years, my husband will start believing what I wrote. You know that happened with a movie on *The House of the Spirits?* When I wrote the book 12 years ago, my relatives were very angry at me. Then the book became very popular, and so they started playing the roles, and now the book has replaced the real memory of the family; they talk as if these things have happened. But the movie is more powerful than the book. As soon as it was released, Meryl Streep and Jeremy Irons became my grandparents!

What would be some advice you would give to someone who'd like to write their own novel or short stories? What would you tell them to do?

Writing short stories is very difficult. I find it much more difficult than a long novel. A short story is closer to poetry; you need inspiration. I can't give any advice, but when I've been teaching, I try to tell my students that this is like training to be an athlete. You are never going to break the record if you don't train every day. There's no way that you will just write the great novel by chance. You have to work, and there is a lot of work involved, daily work. Then I think you have to be very cruel with the editing. Don't have any compassion for what doesn't work, even if you've spent months working on that chapter. Just eliminate it. The best advice I've ever received is cut, cut, cut. You do that in journalism all the time. When you're looking for an adjective, all of a sudden you realize you don't need an adjective. Leave the noun alone. The same thing you can do with a sentence, with a chapter, with a lot of stuff—cut.

It reminds me of something that you wrote about your grandfather. I'd like to talk about him. He was, I think, chastising you for your walking into Neruda's funeral when Neruda died, and he was chastising you for exposing yourself that way to the military leaders at the time. You said something like, "Well, I have to do something, the world is awful," and he said, "The world's always been like this. What are you doing, the world's always been like this." It was a great chastisement.

Yes, he didn't want me to take any risks, but it was a time when you had to. You had to have a position. It was either with the military or against it. I was against, it of course. Although he was a conservative man, he was democratic: He did not like the fact that we had a military coup in Chile, but he didn't want me to be exposed. Also, because I carried a name that was like a neon sign at the time. Being called Allende in those days was really something that you had to watch. So he was very worried about me.

You were actually allowed to practice journalism after the coup formed.

For a while.

So what was it like for you when you finally left?

My life had changed already, the day of the military coup. I think that day I became aware that there is a dimension of violence always present in our lives, and I had failed to see it. I thought that the world was a good place, that people were basically good. Evil was a sort of accident, something that had gone wrong for a while, but it would naturally go back to its natural course, which was goodness. I realized the day of the military coup that it wasn't like that at all. That in our nature and in the society in the world, there is evil all the time, absolute evil some-times. And sometimes that absolute evil takes over in a society. You have to acknowledge—not deny it—and live with it and fight against it. First in your own soul, in order to make a differ-ence, then in the world.

So I had already changed during the first days of the coup. By the time I left Chile, I had lost everything. I realized I had lost my country, my friends, my job, my house, my extended family, and I went to a place where I didn't have any friends or a visa or money or anything. I tried to find a job. Then my husband and my kids reunited with me in Venezuela, and somehow we tried to put a family back together. But you know in Latin America, family is not a nuclear family. A family is something that is supported by a lot of people, by grandmothers and mothers-in-law and all sorts of relatives. We lacked that, and it was hard. Fortunately, in the United States, I have been able to somehow reproduce an extend-ed family. Now we have an open house with a lot of people com-ing in and out, a lot of people in our lives helping each other.

I want to return to your grandfather. You called him Tata? So tell us about your grandfather. He was also a powerful influence, wasn't he?

Yes, because my father disappeared from my life very early. I don't have any memories of my father. My mother went back to live in her father's house. My grandfather was a pragmatic Basque. My grandmother was totally different from him; she was from Castillian origin, not pragmatic at all. She practiced telepa-thy and clairvoyance, and she played with tarot cards and had a three-legged table. My grandfather was fascinated by her, so there must have been something that was wild in his soul. I relat-ed to him with hate and love. Fear and rebelliousness. I was prob-ably the only grandchild that he ever liked or loved, because I reminded him of his wife, my grandmother who had died. He was a powerful influence in my life. Every time that I need to be strong, that I need discipline, that I need to do something that I don't want to do, his spirit comes to me with some tough, stoic, pragmatic idea.

I recall one of the stories you shared in Paula *about your interview with Neruda, when you went down to interview him the first time when you were a journalist. I think his response to you was how can I interview with a journalist like you? You're involved with all your stories.*

He said I was a lousy journalist. Actually, he said, the worst in the country. He said that I could not be objective. I lied all the time. I put myself in the middle of the story, and most probably if I didn't have a story, I would make it up. So why didn't I switch to literature where all those defects were virtues.

What did you think when he told you that?

I thought he was just old and crazy. I had a high opinion of myself at the time. I have changed

Do you really think there's anything such as objective journalism?

No.

I don't either.

I don't think that you can be objective in life, and if you are, there's probably something wrong with you. In everything that one does, one projects oneself. Myself as a writer, why do I choose those stories? Why do I want to talk through those characters? Because I'm exploring something in my soul. This is important to me in one way or another. As a journalist, no matter how objective you try to be, it's your point of view. It's you as a human being. It's your vision, your story.

It's difficult to imagine separating oneself out and saying, Okay, this is my objective journalist self, and this is me over here. I mean, there's no way real to do that. Yet that's what you learn in journalism 101, right? They're still teaching it that way.

They're teaching it because they have to teach it. That's the ethics of the whole thing. But it doesn't work that way.

EPILOGUE

The mystery of the creative process comes alive through the words of Isabel Allende, who is refreshingly direct and candid. Her capacity to enter the experience of her life and bring back a vivid accounting mirrors what is possible for each of us in our creative journey. She reminds us that deep within there is a hidden reservoir of knowledge that can be tapped through being quiet. This is the source of creativity, and it is available if we are willing to find the place of silence and solitude where it can emerge. In a profound and mysterious way, it's not what we know that propels us forward to creativity, but what we don't know that moves us. It is this "don't know" place that allows us to create something original, fresh, and new.

CHAPTER SIX

▼ ▼ ▼

Creativity: A Mysterious Process

Mihály Csikszentmihályi, with Michael Toms

PROLOGUE

*C*reativity is what makes life worth living. The charge we feel
when we're in the flow of creating is unlike anything else.
*How do we realize our optimal creativity? What could we do in
our daily life to be more creative? Can creativity actually make
our life more satisfying and fulfilling? The answer to these and
other questions serve as our focus in this dialogue with Mihály
Csikszentmihályi (pronounced* chick-sent-me-hi*). A professor of
psychology at the University of Chicago and author of the bestselling book,* Flow: The Evolving Self and Creativity, *Mihály
Csikszentmihályi spent five years interviewing a select group of a
hundred exceptional individuals in an effort to make more under-
standable the mysterious process by which men and women come
up with new ideas and things, how the creative process unfolds*

over a lifetime, and what conditions encourage or hinder the generation of original ideas.

🔥   🔥   🔥

MICHAEL TOMS: Mihály, is there a definition of creativity?

MIHALY CSIKSZENTMIHALYI: One that most people usually agree on is that creativity has to be a new idea or a product that is socially acceptable and valued and which is brought to fruition. That's creativity with a big *C.* Creativity that changes the culture. Then we can talk also about creativity, which is a more personal experience that a person has in the way they approach life, in the way that you experience life, with originality, openness, freshness. That is something different in a sense that they overlap, but it is creativity with a small *c,* the personal creativity that makes life enjoyable, but does not necessarily result in fame or renown or success.

So literally everyone can be creative.

That is true.

So why aren't we?

Because there's just so much market for new ideas or new ways of doing things. There's a tremendous inertia and conservatism in any culture, and it has to be like that. I mean, we can't invent new things all the time; we have to have someone state the true ways of doing things. We are conservative by nature. Children like the same food. They don't want to experiment with new things. They like the same fairy tales over and over. I think, to some extent, that we need that tradition and security, and then we also need creativity, but we can't do it all the time. In many fields, unfortunately, there's just not enough of a market for new ideas.

One of the interesting ideas things that you brought out in your book Creativity *was the fact that it's not just someone being alone, being creative, but there's a synergy of forces and circumstances—and, you used the term* luck—*that makes a person creative. So it's not this idea, this myth we have about the single individual loner out there being creative, but there's something else involved.*

Luck was the most often-mentioned reason that these people who are very creative and well known in their fields—people such as Jonas Salk, inventor of the polio vaccine; or Linus Pauling—they all said luck is what made them achieve what they did. By that they meant several things. They meant that good genes are luck, having a background that allows you to focus on a particular domain of knowledge—that's partly luck. Being at the right time and right place is luck.

For instance, in the case of Pauling, he was one of the first generations of chemists who was exposed to quantum mechanics in the early twenties, when it just came over from Europe. He saw the similarity between the behavior of particles in the subatomic level and the molecular level. He said, Hey, maybe I can apply this to chemistry, and he had this window of opportunity of maybe a year or two in which he could do that. Otherwise, somebody else would have done it. He had been a young student and he used that opportunity. Of course, he had to know enough to recognize that this possibility was there, but in many ways luck does play a big role in transforming this creativity with a small c to creativity with a capital C. That is the creativity that changes the culture. For that you need luck, but everybody can have creativity at the personal level and make their own life more interesting and more like a process of discovery.

Also, one of the aspects you coupled with luck was perseverance. Many of the people mentioned their ability to hang in there during tough times.

Even in normal times. You know, each one of these, whether you're a poet or a sculptor or a scientist or a businessman, they say their everyday work involves a small amount of wild, marvelous ideas and a lot of perseverance and hard work. Many of them use that famous idea that Thomas Edison used: Creativity is one percent inspiration and 99 percent perspiration. I think it's true. You have to be able to transform those wild ideas into something that will stand up, and that's hard work.

Another interesting aspect of what you came up with in your research with these people was the frequent mention of having idle time, time on their hands. That was an important aspect of creativity.

Right, for several reasons. For instance, Robertson Davies, the Canadian author, said that one of the most important things in his life was something very trivial—it's being able to take a nap every day after lunch for 20 minutes. That's for two reasons. One is that by developing a schedule that's under your control, you're not being flung around by life, as he puts it. You know that you're not always jumping to someone else's tune. You develop your own rhythm of work and rest. That's one thing. The other thing is that it's during idle time that ideas have a chance to recombine in new ways, because if we think consciously about solving a problem or writing a book, then we are sitting there forcing our ideas to move in a lock step and straight line. Probably what comes out is not very new or original. For original ideas to come about, you have to let them kind of percolate under the level of consciousness in a place where we have no way to make them obey our own desires or our own directions. So they find their way. The combinations, random combinations, are those that are driven by forces we don't know about, and it's true that something new may come up. Not when we try to push them directly.

So it's like the aphorism: Don't just do something, sit there.

Right. That's a good one. In one famous computer company, somebody made a lot of discoveries, and this firm lost several million dollars because they did not install a $14,000 shower in this man's office because all his good ideas came when he's showering. So they lost all these ideas when he moved to a new firm that had a shower, and all these great ideas kept coming out. So for some people it's the shower, some people get it driving, others walking the dog.

Mihály, is there a creative personality, as such? Certain aspects of the creative personality that we might know about?

It seems as if people who are able to transform the domain in which they work have certain similarities in the way their personalities are put together. What I call that is complexity of their personality, which means that each one of us has several possible options in terms of personality. We can either be extroverts and enjoy people, but then feel kind of anxious when we're alone. Or we can be introverted, which means that we like solitude but can't handle people.

In many other dimensions of personality, we are either masculine or feminine. Or we're cooperative, competitive, et cetera, et cetera. Whereas creative people, I find, have the ability to use the full range of this separate dimension so that they have masculine and feminine traits. Both men and women have some of the strengths of the opposite gender. They can be introverted when they have to be, when they have to work. They love being alone and working, but they also love being with people when that helps their work so that they can get the information that is very important to know in all of these fields, to know what other people are thinking and doing and so forth.

Carl Jung also recognized that what we usually have is being developed in one part of our personality, and we repress the opposite part. That becomes our shadow. To become fully functioning as an adult, you have to recognize what your shadow is and be able to integrate that into your repertoire of behaviors. With these people, it seems in many ways that their shadow is integrated into their light side in a way that is unusual for most people.

Also, one of the things that I notice when you mention the dimensions of complexity is that these people seem to encompass extremes. There's a paradox here, that they're realistic and yet can dwell in fantasy.

They're playful and responsible at the same time. Most of these people are both very rebellious and iconoclastic. They like to break rules; they like to break tradition. That's true, but on the other hand, they're also very traditional. Whatever they accomplish is based on the accomplishments of previous generations. They take those accomplishments very seriously, and, at the same time, they are willing to go beyond and break the limits of what has been done or known in the past. You have to be traditional, and you have to be iconoclastic. All of these polarities are somehow integrated in their work. I think that, for instance, has important implications, let's say for child rearing. We have an idea that our children should be either one thing or another. You have to be very vigorous, but not let your fantasies run around. You have to be very macho masculine if you are a boy, and feminine if you are a girl. We run the risk by doing that to pigeonhole our children into half-people—I mean, made up of many halves of what humans could be. I think certainly if we wanted to treat these individuals' creativity, one of the implications is that we have to build on all the strengths that children have spontaneously and not make them ashamed of using the parts that we think are not important, because it could be very important.

Mihály, you've been studying creativity for many, many years. I'm wondering about your research, your work, your focus in this area. How has that affected your own creativity? How has that worked for you?

Luckily, I have been able to remain quite objective, I hope. I haven't let it run my life in a sense of being self-conscious. Oh, now, if I do this, I'm not creative. If I do that, it's creative. I think none of the people I interviewed, these hundreds of people, were trying consciously. There are some creative people who have assumed the persona of the genius. They were just in love with what they were doing, and they want to do it well, and that's it.

How can you be objective when you're right in it? You're right there in the process. You have to be a part of it.

I guess that wasn't even the right word. What I meant is that I'm not thinking that, Oh, if I do this, how can I learn and apply it in my own life—that kind of thing. I'm just doing it because it's fun, it's important, and I love to do it.

That really is in some ways the characteristics of many of the people that you talked to. That it's not for the result of the work they're doing, or for money or for fame. It's for just the sheer joy and exhilaration of doing it, isn't it?

I would say that if there is one characteristic that is common to all of this, that's certainly it. The other one is the curiosity and interest in life that these people show, but that's part of the same thing, actually. It's interesting. Motivation and curiosity are very tightly interwoven, and that's the main trait that they all share.

I can identify with it because I really enjoy talking to people like yourself. I'm curious about what you're doing and what you're about—it's a wonderful process.

It is. The thing is that life offers so many of these opportunities. I mean, some people don't like to talk to people, but they like to work with machines and computers or something. Others with plants, others, well, you know, it's limitless. There's so much.

You know, most of us are so creative at holding ourselves back from experiencing that wonderful process of creativity. Why are we so good at that?

I think we children have them spontaneously, this interest and curiosity and excitement about life. Unfortunately, sooner or later, it's beaten out of them in a sense, metaphorically speaking.

It's almost educated out of them, too.

That's right. I think schools, unfortunately—at least mass education the way we have been doing for the last 150 years or so—is not ideal for encouraging the curiosity and this kind of self-directed interest that children have.

So part of being creative and being in a creative flow is having a sense of wonder, having a sense of awe at life around us, isn't it?

Awe is a great word. I mean, the scientists are saying that they are getting in touch with the mystery of what makes the universe go. That's awesome, and they feel they are getting closer to that. Mathematicians feel the awe of the order of quantities, the musicians are in awe of the harmony of sound, the poets are in awe of the power of words. I think *awe* is a good word. Somehow they have that. It would be nice if more people could feel that. I think it's possible, but it's kind of ended up being taken for granted—life. We think that the little cubicle in which we live and the little routine that we learn is life. Then that's it. There's nothing interesting outside of that. That is a sad situation—I mean, for those who live that way, I think.

Also, one of the aspects of these creative people you talked with was they all were divergent thinkers. They all seem to be able to hold a diversity of ideas to be able to explore many possibilities.

Right. Our education is based on convergence thinking, which is to point people toward the same solution, and there's one right solution. No matter where you start, you have to get to that one solution. So that's the convergence. Divergent thinkers start with something completely obvious, and they see a number of possibilities in it. For instance, when Einstein was asked why he came up with the theory of relativity, he said because I couldn't understand the old physics. It's not that he couldn't understand it, but what was obvious to others was not obvious to him.

So instead of converging on one right solution, you diverge through possibilities. One of those possibilities may be very important and interesting. That's how you generate discoveries— by asking many questions. Or like some of the people have this tactic. One of the persons I interview subconsciously, whenever somebody tells him that something is so and so, he says, Well, let me think of it as being the opposite. So he turns every statement he has into the opposite and sees how it looks from that other 180 degrees reversed. You know, I'm not sure that helps a lot, but it is part of this divergent thinking process. Not taking things for granted necessarily, I mean.

It brings to mind the idea that perhaps t real creativity is not in the answers, but in the questions we ask.

A lot of people have said that, including Einstein. I think there's a lot in that.

Does creativity get better as we age? As we get older, does it expand?

Well, that's one interesting thing that I found. Although you would expect that these people in their eighties and nineties had certain faculties declining, and they couldn't be as fast. Their memories maybe weren't as good. They made some mistakes, if they were scientists, with calculations and so forth. Despite that, there were more positive stories and positive explanations as to how their creativity has changed over time than negative ones. For instance, one thing that surprised me a lot was that many of these people say that now they are much more able to take risks. At first I thought that was just kind of whistling in the dark, but actually it's true. I mean, in the life of these people comes a time when they say, Hey, you know, we don't have to worry as much about the opinion of my peers as before. I have proven something. Now I can try something really on the fringe and see whether it works or not. You still have to, if you want to keep being creative, you still have to be self-critical. You still have to use the evaluation of your field to decide whether what you're doing makes sense or not, but you can run more risks.

There is a feeling, also, of being able to move into areas that you hadn't moved before or connecting between fields that seem disparate, but you begin to see similarities with experience, with age. Many of these people feel that they're very satisfied by being able to help and to be involved in more social, political issues than before. So they expand the reach of their activities to move beyond the kind of narrow specialization and so forth. So yes, there is very good news in the way these people are able to use their creativity.

Mihály, I asked you about the fact that many people are creative who we don't know about. What about that?

That is true. According to the last census, there were almost half a million Americans who say that their profession was artist. A half a million people. Yet if you ask a representative sample of Americans to name artists they know, living artists they know, the average is less than one. The majority mentioned Picasso, who has been dead for 30 years. When you look at the duration, you realize that out of those half a million, there are probably a heck of a lot of good artists, but how are they going to be creative if nobody knows their work and their work is not going to be saved and is not going to enter the tradition of the culture.

Sometimes you have to die in order to get famous, don't you? That helps sometimes.

Look at van Gogh. He sold one painting during his whole lifetime.

Probably there were thousands of painters like van Gogh in his lifetime. Most of their work didn't make much sense to the next generation. Van Gogh's work, which was so tortured and so full of anxiety, happened to coincide with the spirit of the times racked by World War I, where all certainties were destroyed. Then people recognized in these paintings a disturbed person, something that moved and spoke to them.

They saw something of themselves reflected there.

At the same time, many of his contemporaries who were probably as original and as good or even better than he did not fill a need in the spiritual marketplace, so to speak. So their work we don't know about. So that's why creativity, as we understand it, is merely constituted both by the supply side and the demand side, in a sense. There has to be an artist to supply the novelty, but there also has to be an audience who needs that and who can recognize it and can respond to it. So that if we don't have a creative period in some art or science, it may not be that there are not many creative individuals having good ideas. It may be that we don't have an eco-chain, so to speak, that could reflect these ideas and make something out of them so that it becomes part of the culture. So if we think of creativity as a systems property rather than an individual property, then it's much easier to see how to increase it in a sense. Or make it more likely to occur by working, not just on the level of the person, but on the level of the social system that can use ideas, recognize support, etc.

So a supportive environment is extremely important to allow creativity to flourish, right?

That is essential, yes. I mean in this whole huge country, there's one institution that recognizes creativity in science in high schools, the Westinghouse prize. Now there are hundreds of kids in high school whose work gets recognized and publicized during the year. So many good high schools around the country prepare the students to come up with new ideas for this one prize. Suppose the Westinghouse prize wasn't there. There would still be these creative kids around, but they wouldn't be doing anything, and we wouldn't know about it, and they wouldn't be encouraged. What if, instead of this one, you had ten of those. Suddenly, creativity in high school in science would become a much bigger thing than it is now. I think this is true in every field.

It makes me think of how Congress is recently taking away the money from the National Endowment for the Arts and National Endowment for Humanities, which are agencies basically set up to encourage creativity.

It's important. The one thing that the National Endowment for the Arts may not have done that would make it much more acceptable is that, see, certain domains develop away from the rest of the culture, and they become kind of self-reinforcing enclaves where things happen that don't really match what the rest of the people want. To some extent, modern art has run into that problem. It's not enough to have money to give artists, but also to give attention and criticism, and the criticism has to be sensible as part of the culture as a whole. Not just as modern art, separate from the rest of the world. I have that sense, you know, that modern art has become a little bit too isolated, and, therefore, the field of art is not as vitally connected to the rest of the culture.

It brings up the question of how so often the leading edge in any field, whether it be art or music or science, is often not part of the dominant mainstream thinking. It's often on the margins and outside. You really have to look beyond. You can't just say, Well, it's a dominant culture, it has to agree with the dominant culture, right? You can't just say that.

That was eye-opening for me to look at—for instance, the Renaissance in Florence, where so many great works of visual art—architecture, sculpture painting—were created in the early 15th century, and how incredibly involved the whole city was in that program. For instance, when they were building, trying to build the dome over the cathedral of Florence, it was a job that no architect could do. For 80 years, they had a competition to come up with a drawing to build a dome—for 80 years. Every year, practically every week, there were people in the city trying to come up with ideas and suggestions. This was part of the everyday conversation in the city.

Finally, Brunelleschi, the architect, ended up finding a solution and built a dome, and the whole city knew what an incredible feat this was. It was something in every other work or bad period, the artist being supported, criticized by bankers, by heads of the unions, the guilt sometimes by the bishops. So it was the whole community who cared. It wasn't just money, but it was care and concern and a feeling that these people were on our side. We were doing this together. We were in it together, and we were doing it together. I think music 200 years later—the great flowering of music in Germany, Austria—that was also supported by the bishops, the courts of the Eszterhazy.

You had Hayden and Beethoven working for them, and all these princes who cared about music because that was part of the court's reputation, to have good musicians. So they chose musicians carefully. They paid attention to what they played, and it mattered to them. They cared. Now we don't care that much about art. I mean we want artists. We want museums, but it's like they play, you know it's like sandboxes when they can play on their own, but it's not really part of serious life.

So how do we bring it back? Do you have some suggestions or insights as to how to bring the creative process back into the culture so that it's not split off?

If you just look at which art forms are part of the consciousness of the culture, you would have to conclude that these days it's movies, and it's popular music. Where the action is in terms of voicing the concerns, voicing the emotional and existential problems of our time. I'm not a great fan of modern music myself, but I must recognize that there is something happening there that is very meaningful to the younger generations. Whereas traditional, classical music composed now is mostly done at universities in departments of music, and not many people hear that. We do have a culture in the process of being formed, and there's a lot of creativity in the movies, there's a lot of creativity in the new media—virtual reality and all that. These new forms that are developing, whether they will create a civilization similar to renaissance Florence or Athens, I don't know.

In our culture, so often creativity is associated with how much money it's able to generate. For example, a film is creative if it generates a lot of income or revenue. Many artists, in the area of music, certainly popular music and film, are seen as creative if they're really successful making a lot of money. So much of our relationship to creativity in this society is translated relative to money. Yet we both know that creativity is far beyond just the equation of money.

In this context, it's interesting. I don't know if you've heard about it, but in the country my family comes from, in Hungary, not so long ago there was an interesting law that went into effect called the Garbage Tax Law. The garbage tax was levied on any work of culture that sold a lot. So if you sold a lot of records, the Beatles were a big revenue source for the garbage tax. That money went to subsidize string quartets and the money that you levied on mystery writers like Tom Clancy, or something like Stephen King's books would go to subsidize poetry. I thought that was ingenious, but I don't know that these kind of artificially imposed changes will lead us to where we want to be. I think somehow people have developed better tastes for what they're willing to pay for.

I can imagine revenue from the sale of tickets to Arnold Schwarzenegger's Terminator 2 *going to support independent filmmakers, something like that. That's a great idea.*

Even during the Renaissance and the Middle Ages or the age of the Greeks, the artistic production wasn't done necessarily just for pure reasons. They wanted to build big palaces to impress the people and big cathedral in Florence so they could put to shame the cathedrals of Sienna, or some other city. So it wasn't monetary, but it was political; it was status. A lot of the arts were supported by pretty base reasons, basically, yet they transcended that thing. I think there are some money-making films now that transcend the purely monetary thing. There are some movies, even blockbusters, that really change the way we experience things.

Give me an example from your perspective.

This may be childish, but I did enjoy the *Star Wars* movies, especially when they first came out. I thought they were greatly liberating in some ways.

They're archetypal in many ways.

Yes. They have that archetypal quality—I'm thinking about blockbusters now. Of course there were many others that were less successful financially but that had both qualities, I think.

I think that George Lucas actually admitted that much of his inspiration had come from Joseph Campbell and his readings on mythology. There were so many mythological themes within the Star Wars *trilogy. In the summer of 1996, one of the blockbuster films was* Independence Day, *and apparently one of the reasons it was so successful, psychologists tell us, was its archetypal quality. People want to identify with their fellow human beings, and this is an opportunity around the theme of a film like* Star Wars *or* Independence Day. *Everybody discovers their oneness with others on the planet.*

I always thought during the Cold War period that one of the ways to resolve the conflict between us and Russia was to build a kind of artificial spaceship and bury it somewhere in the jungles of Africa with a message that the earth would be invaded in 2010, then discover the plan and say, "Oh my God, we have to get together." I think there is so much that unites us, and it's so silly, too.

I was really impressed by the range and diversity of people that you selected for this five-year survey that you did the interviews with. How did you go about selecting people?

I wanted to get people who had been creative for a while, not just a flash in the pan at one period in their life. So that dictated that I should get older people who had a whole history of achievements over time. So I started asking for nominations, first from colleagues and experts in the field, then from my collaborators, my graduate students. We would sit down and sift through and try to evaluate who really has changed the most—let's say, physics and poetry and so forth and who was also over 60 years old. Then we would write to these people. I would explain what I was trying to do and ask whether they would consent to be interviewed and be there for a couple of hours. So I sent about 300 letters, of which about one-third were accepted. The other two-thirds were either too busy or refused for a variety of reasons, or they were afraid that by talking too much about the roots of their creativity, they would kind of injure the sources of their inspiration. They would lose it.

Maybe jinx themselves in some way.

Since then, I've thought a lot about why that is so. When you look at the beginning of how a great novelist begins a story, starts to write a book, very often the beginning, the idea, the germ of the idea, is very trivial and very simple. Yet, if you want to make it into a great book, you have to take that simple idea seriously. You have to believe that this is the most important thing in the world at this point. So it's through the struggle of developing the germ of an idea that you create a good story, a good book. But at the beginning, it's almost like a Potemkin village. You're creating something out of nothing. If you knew, if you really had to face up to how silly or trivial that germ of idea is at the beginning, you would give up. You would say, Oh well, this is never going to fly. In a sense, an artist very often has to trick himself or herself to believe that this is the voice of the muse, this is a story that I just have to tell. It's the greatest story, even though it's not. Then you make it through by working hard. That's my interpretation of why artists are reluctant to talk.

But sometimes it may not just be mental trickery, but it may also just be the drive from within that I have to do this. It can come from a deeper level, can't it?

Yes. The point, I think, is that the drive is there, but it's through hard work that the drive pushes you. That this trivial idea will become something beautiful. Because as we talk about *Star Wars*, I mean the idea of *Star Wars* is an old one. It's a mythical archetype, and it's been told so many times. So when you start thinking, Hey, let's do a movie about this, at first it sounds like, why bother? But then if you take it seriously and you begin to really put your effort and your energy into it, then you could create a work that is awesome. But you can short-circuit that process if you know too much about the beginning, because then you say it's been done.

You know, there are many important insights that came out of your research work, but perhaps the most salient point, the message of all the people that you talked with, was the statement that you, too—meaning all of us—can spend our lives doing what we love to do. That really is the major message, isn't it? Because most us think we can't do that, you know?

That's right. It's because we associate creativity with this unique position in the culture. It's true that we can't all be Einsteins, we can't all be Beethovens, so if we think of creativity as that success and recognition, then it's true we can't do it. But each one of us can experience the feeling of discovery that these people had. We may not have the luck to be able to occupy the niche of an Einstein, but we can certainly appreciate the mystery of the universe, the beauty or harmony of how nature is put together, like fantastic clockwork. All of those things we can learn about, we can participate in, we can enjoy, and at that level, that kind of creativity is what really makes life full and worth living.

Yes. So hopefully, we can start to do that, if we're not doing it now.

And one can start with small steps. Darwin, who revolutionized our understanding of biology and evolution, started collecting bugs. He was so excited one day when he discovered three big beetles that he wanted to take all three, but only two fit in his hands. So he popped one in his mouth, and he ran home with three beetles—one in his mouth and two in his hands. That kind of excitement is what 50 years later has altered the theory of evolution. The excitement, the interest, is there, and we can all share in that.

✶   ✶   ✶

EPILOGUE

In this dialogue, Csikszentmihályi provides an overall context with which to hold creativity. Even though there is mystery, certain traits contribute to being creative, such as truly enjoying what you are doing. A sense of play and adventure, even in the most difficult tasks, seems common to most creative persons. The attainment of fame or making money is not important. Rather, it is loving what you do plus finding meaning and purpose in your work that feeds the creative process. He suggests looking at a problem from as many different viewpoints as possible. Divergent thinking is a key to creativity. Be surprised by something every day. When your interest is sparked, follow it. Wake up in the morning with a specific goal to accomplish, no matter how mundane. There are myriad ways to be creative. As you nurture you own creativity, life will naturally become more meaningful, satisfying, and enjoyable.

RECOMMENDED READING

The Artist's Way: A Spiritual Path to Higher Creativity,
by Julia Cameron

The Artist's Way: Morning Pages Journal, by Julia Cameron

The Art of Creativity, by Wilferd Peterson

Banana Rose, by Natalie Goldberg

Creating from the Spirit: Living Each Day As a Creative Act,
by Dan Wakefield

*Creativity: Flow and the Psychology of Discovery and
Invention,* by Mihály Csikszentmihályi

*Creators on Creating: Awakening and Cultivating the
Imaginative Mind,* edited by Frank Barron, Alfonso Montuori
and Anthea Barron

Drawing the Light from Within, by Judith Cornell

Eva Luna, by Isabel Allende

The Evolving Self: A Psychology for the Third Millennium,
by Mihály Csikszentmihályi

Flow: The Psychology of Optimal Experience, by Mihály Csikszentmihályi

The House of the Spirits, by Isabel Allende

The Infinite Plan, by Isabel Allende

Long Quiet Highway, by Natalie Goldberg

Looking for the Faces of God, by Deena Metzger

The Money Drunk: 90 Days to Financial Freedom, by Julia Cameron and Mark Bryan

Of Love and Shadows, by Isabel Allende

Paula, by Isabel Allende

The Vein of Gold: A Journey to Your Creative Heart, by Julia Cameron

What Dinah Thought, by Deena Metzger

Wild Mind: Living the Writer's Life, by Natalie Goldberg

Write from the Heart, by Hal Bennett

Writing Down the Bones, by Natalie Goldberg

Writing for Your Life: Discovering the Story of Your Life's Journey, by Deena Metzger

NEW DIMENSIONS FOUNDATION

Since its inception in 1973, New Dimensions Foundation has presented lecture series, live events and seminars; published books, sponsored educational tours, and launched a major periodical. Created to address the dramatic cultural shifts and changing human values in our society, New Dimensions has become an international forum for some of the most innovative ideas expressed on the planet. Its principal and best-known activity is New Dimensions Radio, an independent producer of radio dialogues and other programming.

During the past 20 years, many of this century's leading thinkers and social innovators have spoken through New Dimensions. The programming supports a diversity of views from many traditions and cultures. Now is a time for transformative learning and for staying open to all possibilities. We must constantly be willing to review and revise what we are creating. New Dimensions fosters the goals of living a more healthy life of mind, body, and spirit while deepening our connections to self, family, community, environment, and planet.

New Dimensions is a rare entity in the world of media—a completely independent, noncommercial radio producer. Primary support comes from listeners. Members of "Friends of New Dimensions" (FOND) are active partners in a community of hope and grounded optimism as we celebrate the human spirit and explore new ideas, provocative insights, and creative solutions across the globe over the airwaves.

You too can play an invaluable part in this positive force for change by becoming a member of (FOND) and supporting the continued production and international distribution of New Dimensions Radio programming. (See the next page for more details.)

Books, Audios, and More from New Dimensions

(Available through Hay House)

BOOKS

Buddhism in the West—The Dalai Lama and other contributors
Money, Money, Money—Jacob Needleman and other contributors
The Power of Meditation and Prayer—Larry Dossey, M.D.,
    and other contributors
Roots of Healing—Andrew Weil, M.D., and other contributors
The Soul of Business—Charles Garfield and other contributors
The Well of Creativity—Jean Houston and other contributors

AUDIOS

(All of the audios below feature New Dimensions Radio co-founder
Michael Toms interviewing some of the foremost thinkers and social
innovators of our time.)

The Art of Soul Work—Thomas Moore
Authentic Power—Gary Zukav
Future Medicine—Daniel Goleman
Healing from the Inside Out—Bernie Siegel, M.D.
Healing with Spirit—Caroline Myss, Ph.D.
The Heart of Spiritual Practice—Jack Kornfield
Live Long and Feel Good—Andrew Weil, M.D.
Make Your Dreams Real—Barbara Sher
Medicine, Meaning, and Prayer—Larry Dossey, M.D.
Messages of the Celestine Prophecy—James and Salle Redfield
A New Approach to Medicine—Andrew Weil, M.D.
The New Millennium—Jean Houston
Roots of Healing—Andrew Weil, M.D., and others
Sacred Odyssey—Ram Dass
The Wisdom of Joseph Campbell—Joseph Campbell

CALENDAR

Wise Words: Perennial Wisdom from the New Dimensions Radio Series

---

To order the products above, please call Hay House at 800-654-5126.

We hope you enjoyed
this Hay House/New Dimensions book.
If you would like to receive a free catalog featuring
additional Hay House books and products, or if you would like
information about the Hay Foundation, please contact:

Hay House, Inc.
P.O. Box 5100
Carlsbad, CA 92018-5100

(800) 654-5126
(800) 650-5115 (fax)

Please visit the Hay House Website at: **www.hayhouse.com**
and the New Dimensions Website at: **www.newdimensions.org**